I0789388

FROM BELIEF TO TRUTH – FROM TRUTH TO WISDOM

BY

ENDALL BEALL

DEDICATION

This book is dedicated to the teachers who left humanity the information required for how to transcend being simply human and becoming more than what humanity thinks it is; Siddhartha Guatama (Buddha), Jesus, Friedrich Nietzsche and don Juan Matús. Humanity owes all these men a great debt of gratitude that I hope this book reveals.

TABLE OF CONTENTS

ACKNOWLEDGEMENTS

Acknowledgement is due all the teachers for the advancement of human consciousness and the teachings they left for humanity. Their gift to humanity transcends any other acknowledgements that I can offer.

INTRODUCTION

The book you have in your hand may be one of the most valuable and dangerous books every offered to mankind. I do not make this assessment based on any notions of personal grandiosity, ego arrogance, or as a crass sensationalist sentence just to sell a book. Once the reader digests the material in this book, then this assertion should be patently clear, for it is the information itself that will support my claim.

Throughout the ages humanity has taken its direction for cultural growth, for the most part, from the intellectuals of our species. At the hands of these intellectual elite, we have seen our species move from the ranks as farmers and herders, servants and slaves, through what we have been educated into believing is the advancement of civilization. Our progression has grown from communities used to support the primary temples of the ancient gods and their created priesthoods, into city states, into large metropolitan areas, empires, royal fiefdoms and territories (also ruled by self-appointed elite), which grew into nation states; through the Renaissance into the beginning of technological inventions like the printing press and the creation of engines to refine warfare, through the industrial revolution, the electronic era and into today's technological wonderland.

Through this progression we have been given many brilliant pieces of art and music, grand architecture and building feats of roads, bridges and dams, culminating into all our modern creature comforts like running water in our homes, central heating and air conditioning (in the most well to do parts of the world), and a burgeoning technology that our species can scarcely keep up with as new innovations are cranked out on an almost weekly basis of constant change and innovation.

Amidst all this advancement and innovation, the one thing that has remained in suspended animation, still awaiting to blossom on the branches of the tree of humanity, is wisdom. Regardless of the control by the intellectual elite who pride themselves on all the books they write and fill with their postulates of intelligence and their scientific mastery of the world, these purported greatest minds of our species have gained no more wisdom than an ox, any more than the average man has gained any wisdom by the tutelage and indoctrination in our controlled classrooms about wisdom.

Our species may possess a lot of knowledge from book learning based on the gathering and memorization of presumed facts, but knowledge of this nature is not wisdom. Knowledge and technological advancement throughout the ages has not taught humanity a single thing about being human or what it can be. The acts of inhumanity throughout the ages stand as the testimony to this. Man's inhumanity to man is what casts its greatest shadow over both our cultures and our psyches as a species, and we are still inhumane today, despite our own personal illusions that we are not.

There are billions of people around this planet who are seeking answers, who are seeking a better way to live without all this destructiveness, mayhem, war and avarice for power by these selfsame intellectual elite who can only think of ruling the world. Their desire is to keep all of humanity in ignorant subjugation, being nothing more than mind-controlled slaves, living fruitless lives to support the systems that only enslave them further. These intellectual elite have been very successful in this effort. In fact, their success has been so profound, their cognitive con game so sublime, that humanity doesn't even know that it is enslaved, but actually *thinks* it is free, living in the perceptual illusion woven by these intellectual elite to deceive an entire species.

The control by the intellectual classes has created monopolies, starting with religions, then graduating over the ages into governments, and now controls the financial and banking systems worldwide, the educational systems, the publishing houses that print only what they find acceptable to sell to the masses to keep their program for world domination hidden behind superficial distractions, and they control the media of all kinds through magazines, newspapers, TV and movies.

At first gloss, reading the previous paragraph, your first instinct may be that of disbelief and denial, and such a reaction is not unexpected in a world that is supported only through belief and disbelief. Humanity has been intentionally programmed through systems of religious dependencies since the dawn of history, to the dependency on governments and bureaucracies in the present day. These two factions, the religious and the secular, have been at odds with each other for ages, with each side seeking ultimate control over the human herds, and both governed by their own set of elite intellectuals who work tirelessly to steer the masses into their arenas of control. In neither case is true freedom even an option, only dependency, so the only difference is a superficial perceptual one based strictly on belief or disbelief in one or the other. However, this book is not about conspiracy. I have more than capably covered that aspect in my other works.

This book is about moving from beliefs into accepting the truth, and ultimately finding wisdom. For this journey, I am going to draw on the four individuals who taught what I call second cognition awareness, or tried to, to a world operating solely on misperceptions called beliefs. To transcend into wisdom does not require that one be an intellectual, for the intellectuals continue to prove that they have no wisdom with all their gathering of facts and philosophical speculating over the ages of mankind. Some of the greatest wisdom offered mankind came from illiterate people, specifically those the world knows as Buddha, Jesus and the humble Yaqui sorcerer, Don Juan Matús. Within the class of what one may consider an intellectual, we find Friedrich Nietzsche, who has been classified as a philosopher for the simple reason that none of the intellectual philosophers truly understand the ideas he was trying to relate to this day.

What this book will prove is that regardless of the method of teachings for their time, or how they presented such teachings, they all taught the same thing that I have been trying to share and teach humanity about its potential to be something more, to be something greater than the image of itself it has settled for. Where possible, where copyright restrictions disallow it (as with the don

Juan material), I will directly share the words attributed to these people, or in the case of Nietzsche, his own words. The task I have taken upon myself is one of a translator or interpreter, providing the meaning of these men's teachings in layman's terms so anyone can understand the ideas they presented to the world. The primary focus of this volume is to provide humanity, once again, with the messages all these teachers related, to see if, maybe now, humanity has 'the ears to hear' and understand these messages and finally learn wisdom or not. This door to wisdom has stood open for over 2,500 years, yet few have chosen to walk through that door. Are you ready or willing to walk through that door?

1. SUSPENDING BELIEF

Belief is defined by Merriam Webster as:

"1. a state or habit of mind in which trust or confidence is placed in some person or thing

2. something that is accepted, considered to be true, or held as an opinion

: something believed •an individual's religious or political beliefs; especially

: a tenet or body of tenets held by a group •the beliefs of the Catholic Church

3. conviction of the truth of some statement or the reality of some being or phenomenon especially when based on examination of evidence."

A tenet is defined as:

"a principle, belief, or doctrine generally held to be true; especially one held in common by members of an organization, movement, or profession"

The foregoing definitions show that both beliefs and tenets are based on a form of consensus thinking. Beliefs are accepted because they have been passed down through traditions, religious beliefs, because a culture accepts certain beliefs to be true as they are held in common by that particular culture, or because one chooses to adhere to a specific political ideology. Just because these ideas are 'accepted' or 'generally held to be true' does not give these beliefs the weight of truth, they are simply beliefs based on consensus agreement within generally accepted communal ideas. Given this foundation of what beliefs actually *are*, the only definition of a belief upon which this presentation is remotely reliant is the one where the evidence presented from which to draw a logical and reasonable conclusion is weighed of its own accord once presented. For the purpose of this book the reader is going to have to be truly open-minded, and they are going to have to suspend *all* their beliefs based on preconceived notions or opinions to the contrary in order to weigh the evidence I will present in a truly objective manner.

All it takes to create a system of belief is for one person to spread their ideas to others who will accept that belief, which creates the foundations of religions, political ideologies, cultural historical myths and long-lasting traditions. The first premise you are asked to accept is that what you perceive as reality, is in fact, a perceptual illusion based on communal beliefs in many varied forms. I am not saying that our 3D material reality is not real, I am saying that our perception within that material reality is not what we think it is. Based on thousands of years of 'accepted beliefs', our perceptual reality is so riddled with illusions of perception that we do not perceive reality clearly.

In the teachings of Siddhartha Guatama, the Buddha, he taught the principle of *Maya*, which is translated as "deceit or pretense". It is also translated to mean "illusion", particularly where our mental world of perceptions is concerned. Combining these terms, one realizes the premise through which Buddha taught his wisdom is that we live in a "world of perceptual illusion which is based in pretense and deceit".

The first suspension of belief required in taking the evidence I present in the rest of this book under consideration, is relinquish the idea that the teachings I will analyze have anything to do with any ideas of spirituality or religion, but are instead teachings about a *different state of consciousness*, the attainment of which leads to profound wisdom. Because the word spirituality has been corrupted to mean things strictly religious, or having to do with the mystical Divine, we have had to create a new term to identify this different state of cognitive awareness. In order to remove all the connotations with religion or dependency on God or any other outside source on which to rely in order to reach this higher state of cognitive awareness, I coined the term the Second Cognition to define this advanced state of consciousness. To reach this second cognition state of awareness and move away from the mystical connotations that the word spirit invokes in one's mind, we created the term Psoyca to describe the inner self of higher mind that one finds when this process if complete.

Quoting from our book, *Psoyca: Road to the Second Cognition*, a compilation of video transcripts presented on our Gemma Beall Youtube channel:

"Psoyca - Psoyca (sōy-kah) is both an acronym and a word with a broader definition for cognitive advancement. As an acronym, PSOYCA means Personal Sovereignty Over Your Cognitive Advancement. The definition of psoyca:

Psoyca is a word that replaces the word spirit in the vernacular of defining advancing consciousness for the Second Cognition. Psoyca removes all the mystical connotations that the word spirit presents to the study of cognitive advancement. Psoyca references a state of cognitive awareness that acknowledges the higher state of awareness attained when one expands their consciousness to realize that, although we are all individuated consciousnesses, we are also part of an interactive network of other conscious entities that covers the spectrum of alternate dimensions beyond 3D and the universe at large. Psoyca represents a state of consciousness, to which the Second Cognition is only the preliminary step, whereby an individual can expand their cognitive awareness to tap into a multidimensional multiverse by advancing one's personal perceptual abilities beyond the normal five senses to become a participating member in this interactive network of consciousness. Psoyca represents pragmatic cognitive advancement without the reliance on mystical interpretations that the word spirit represents to the first cognition perceptual reality. With the word psoyca, there is absolutely no reliance on any concept of a supernatural higher consciousness.

From here forward in these presentations we are no longer going to use the word spirit or spiritual advancement because by continuing to use the terms, we are still slaves to the first cognition definition of words that denote that we are lesser beings to something greater than ourselves. Psoyca removes this concept of subservience to some illusionary higher power and places our personal sovereignty over our own consciousness squarely where it needs to be, as the personal responsibility of every individual."

Every human being on the planet at this time, is operating in a perceptual world we call the First Cognition. On the road to the second cognition, we all start that path from the standpoint of first cognition understanding and awareness. Buddha's world of *maya* is the first cognition world of illusionary perceptions based on consensus beliefs and opinions. I coined the term second cognition in my book *Willful Evolution*. The first use of the term is in the following context of that book:

"To advance into what people call spiritual understanding, or the second cognition, we have to strip it of all concepts of the supernatural. We also have to strip ourselves of embracing such limiting and subservient concepts that only saints or holy men can achieve it, and this requires advancing beyond what our current level of cognitive awareness presents us with. With a mindset of subservience of any kind, we can never advance into a cosmic realm of equal conscious opportunity. You can never be equal so long as you think you are lesser than anything or anyone else. You will always be a lesser being for the simple reason that you believe such a thing to be true.

What some call the spirit path is basically a willful choice to evolve yourself to the point where you surpass the limitations of our current thinking processes as a species. As Nietzsche wrote, to view humanity from the perspective of the overman, humanity as it currently operates is either laughable or a painful embarrassment. All we have to do is look at human behavior to see that we are a painfully embarrassing species, what with our wars and dramas, territorial and religious imperatives coupled with greed and control. If one takes a seriously objective look at modern mankind, there are very few redeemable qualities overall that we should continue to embrace, yet our species has done the same things over and over again for millennia. Technology and science have not advanced our collective consciousness one whit in the last 10,000 years. So where does the solution lie? It lies within each individual to recognize that as a species we are just not getting it, and it relies on the individual to change themselves and their cognitive awareness in the face of such limited perceptual abilities. What I am talking about is a form of willful evolution, and it is the only way that you can move up from the simple cognitive system that currently controls your mind into a greater cognitive awareness. If you want to see the overman, you have to turn yourself into that being."

With the suspension of preconceived notions and beliefs about mysticism, holiness, God, and the Divine, one arrives at a more pragmatic foundation from which to analyze the evidence provided in the teachings of the four great men I refer to in this body of work. What the reader will see is that, with all of these preconceived beliefs and culturally-programmed assumptions removed, what comes forth as wisdom is arrived at through the process of willful evolution by doing the hard, psychological assessment to rid ourselves of these illusionary beliefs to attain a clearer state of cognitive awareness. There is no mysticism involved in this process, only the commitment to challenge all the illusions you embrace as your beliefs, to see these beliefs for the fallacious assumptions that they are, ultimately to arrive at the truth of a reality that the perceptual illusions before your eyes blind you from perceiving. In order to discover the reality behind the illusions of belief, you must go through a process of willing and critical analysis, not only of the external beliefs you may have about the world, but more importantly, the illusions you have embraced about yourself through the cognitive device called the ego. You are also going to have to suspend any beliefs you think you have about the ego passed on by the likes of Sigmund Freud and other psychologists who have, at best, only conjectured what the ego is. These conjectures about the ego have become an accepted *belief* in the field of Psychology are just another illusion that has been passed into public awareness through consensus agreement of the masses and authoritarian dictatorialism from academia. This is a classic example of how illusions rule our lives and how one who is presumed to be an authority can make the masses believe almost anything based on that presumption of their authority alone.

There have been many studies of comparative religion over the centuries, and all these analyses launch from a foundation of presumed facts, which presumptions themselves are just another form of accepted illusionary beliefs, the primary fault relying in the belief in some God or higher power. To understand the so-called 'mystical' teachings of Buddha, Jesus, Nietzsche or don Juan, we must look at their teachings as a kind of code. There is always a key to solving any code, and what is presented in this book offers the key to open that lock to the door of understanding what they taught, if not immediately realizing what that state of cognitive awareness actually is by experiencing it yourself.

When we can be truly open-minded enough to cast aside perceptions based on consensus assumptions and accepted beliefs, then the doors to insight open to us and we can see things in a new light. Without the correct key to unlock the door to understand the wisdom that these men tried to teach humanity, then the foundation for understanding what they taught is lacking. There is no key to solve the code when, staying locked in our perceptions and beliefs only leaves us constrained to interpret things in an incorrect manner. Everyone knows that if you start with a faulty equation, the results will never come out right at the end. To date, the basis for analyzing these teachings has been all wrong. The preconceived notions about their teachings as either religion or mysticism are the faulty foundation of the equation on which all subsequent analysis has resided, and it is also why these teachings have seemed so mystical and their mystery has never been solved.

With the new foundation offered in this book for a more realistic and critical analysis of these teachings, I invite all scholars, both professional and layman alike, to rethink what you think you know and reassess your *beliefs* to recalculate what these teachings are actually showing humanity and finally arrive at the correct solution to the equation. The rigid adherence to those beliefs and one's rigid denial will always prevent the truth from being seen, no different than the truth of germs being denied for so long because of accepted cultural illusions and belief. This situation is no different than that. New information requires a reassessment of things accepted as *beliefs*, and when necessary, those beliefs must be turned on their heads and eliminated.

2. EXPLANATIONS ON THE EGO – BUDDHA AND THE FALSE SELF

A suspension of belief is necessary to perceive the ego in a different light than the one generally accepted. Aside from the sense of personal identity, which is the core purpose of the ego as a self-identifier, there is an 'attachment' to the ego that overlays our primary identity and creates a false *persona* that convinces all of us that this *persona* is us. The concept of an invasive mind virus is not new. Don Juan taught of this mind virus and defined it in is teachings as 'the predator', which has given humanity its 'mind' for the purpose of feeding on us and depleting our life force or energy. His information on the predators, 'which came from the cosmos', was presented in Carlos Castenada's book, *The Active Side of Infinity* published in 1998, just before Castenada died.

The concept of a mind virus based on Native American traditional beliefs was introduced by Paul Forbes in his 1992 philosophical presentation, *Columbus and the Other Cannibals,* where he called the virus Wetiko, based on the Cree definition of the word. Forbes had his own anti-Capitalist agenda in writing this book, and offered his own philosophical conjecture that the mind virus is evident only in the Europeans who conquered or settled in the Americas. Being Native American, Forbes could definitely be said to have an axe to grind with his conjectures about the mind virus and his anti-European sentiments.

The next person to weigh in on the subject of the mind virus was Paul Levy. Levy wrote two books on the subject, the first of which is now out of print, but the second book, *Dispelling Wetiko: Breaking the Curse of Evil*, takes the concept of the mind virus, based on both Forbes' idea and don Juan's teachings that this parasitic mind virus did in fact come from the stars to infect human consciousness with what Levy called "malignant egophrenia", or ME.

Don Juan taught that the mind virus of the predators had infected all humanity, and it is the symptoms of this virus which plagues humanity and keeps it from advancing on a consciousness level. We have taken the opportunity to call this virus the haypim virus, which is an acronym for HAcker Program In Your Mind, which is actually what this virus is, a parasitic hijacker and manipulator of human consciousness. I covered the topic of the hapiym virus extensively in my book, *The Energetic War Against Humanity: The 6,000 Year War Against Human Cognitive Advancement* for those interested in a full discussion on the matter.

In brief, this parasitic hacker program, the hapiym virus, attaches to our center of personal identity, our primary ego, and overlays it with itself, creating a world of illusion with which it surrounds itself and weaves into our consciousness, making us believe the virus is actually who we really are. It is this world of cognitive illusion created by the virus and sustained by our belief that the virus is who we really are, that all the teachers of the past were talking about when they taught about overcoming or getting rid of the ego, or false self. You will never remove your personal identity, your core ego, but you *can* remove the perceptual lies that this virus has fed you making you believe that the virus *persona* is really you. This false *persona* and the world of illusion called 'beliefs' created by the hapiym virus in your mind is Buddha's *maya*.

The fabricated perceptual world of the hapiym virus is founded on and driven by beliefs. This is the world of the first cognition that controls all human consciousness at this point in our history. The perceptual world of the virus does not separate our external beliefs from our internal beliefs about ourselves. When people adopt a religion or ideology, they generally don't say, for example, "I believe in Feminism" or whatever, they say, "I *am* a Feminist." Through such means of cognitive deception, the virus shapes our personality by making our beliefs define us for the benefit of the hapiym *persona*. We *become* our beliefs. This is the deception of *maya* about which Buddha taught. A very powerful saying attributed to Buddha about this deception is:

*"Believe nothing on the faith of traditions,
even though they have been held in honor for many
generations and in diverse places. Do not believe
a thing because many people speak of it. Do not
believe on the faith of the sages of the past. Do not
believe what you yourself have imagined,
persuading yourself that a God inspires you.
Believe nothing on the sole authority of your*

What must be noted in this passage is what is being challenged – *beliefs*! The final advice is to learn to believe in yourself based upon your own experiences and judgment of what is best for you, not relying on any of those things noted to make those personal assessments or self-judgments. Every belief is therefore suspect if it comes from any secondhand source of knowledge until proven true through one's own research and experiences, especially if those ideas are adopted based on the reliance of presumed authority figures. This is the path of willful evolution, the road to the second cognition and full psoyca awareness, or personal enlightenment.

What I have presented thus far may very well challenge your own perception of reality, but it doesn't make the reality I present in the alternative untrue. Everyone's perceptual reality is based on psychological conditioning, whether that conditioning comes from cultural programming, religious programming or political programming. Everything we think we know has been indoctrinated into us from the time we were born by one authority figure or another, from our parents to our final teachers in life. We accept all this conditioning and the hapiym virus creates its world of illusion around these conditioned beliefs. We are little more than a collection of accepted facts and labels plugged into us by one authority figure or another all our lives. We are not who we think we are, we are only a pale vestige of who we really are, controlled by the hapiym *persona* ego and its world of deception and illusion. Of this situation, Buddha taught:

> *"Believe nothing merely because you have been told it. Do not believe what your teacher tells you merely out of respect for the teacher. But whatever, after due examination and analysis, you find to be kind, conducive to the good, the benefit, the welfare of all beings - that doctrine, believe and cling to, and take it as your guide."*

In light of the explanations I have provided, can you detect any whiff of mysticism in these two profound and insightful sayings? Do you find any religious overtones given what he stated about not believing what one imagines or persuades themselves that some God or higher source is the basis for their beliefs? Is there anything hard to understand about these sayings that my pragmatic explanations don't clarify?

The path to the second cognition and psoyca awareness, what Buddha called Nirvana, is a personal quest based on the deepest kind of soul searching to eradicate all the false beliefs created by the hapiym virus that we have been convinced is reality. This false reality is just as the character Morpheus stated in *The Matrix* film, it is the world which has been pulled over our eyes to keep us from seeing the truth. The greatest truth this false world of perceptions and beliefs hides from us is the truth about who we really are. In regard to this path, Buddha taught:

"Believe nothing, no matter where you read it, or who said it, no matter if I have said it, unless it agrees with your own reason and your own common sense."

"Doubt everything. Find your own light."

"No one saves us but ourselves. No one can and no one may. We ourselves must walk the path."

What these sayings reveal to us that only we, as individuals, can grow ourselves out of this world of first cognition illusion through the process of thoroughly investigating from whence we got all of our beliefs. If what you think you know and believe doesn't stand up to close investigative scrutiny, then it must be let go as nothing more than a cognitive perceptual illusion, a phantom that has no substance aside from our acceptance and sustaining it as a belief because it brings us mental comfort. By embracing these illusionary beliefs and feeding them, we only feed the illusion of the false hapiym *persona* itself. When we are confronted with a truth that runs contrary to what the false ego has adopted as part of its personality, it creates within us a fear reaction called cognitive dissonance. The false ego rebels at the thought that its belief is wrong and it creates a great sense of anxiety inside us. This negative emotional reaction is what prevents most people from walking the road of willful evolution because it is fraught with fear as we each must erode this world of illusion that we believe is us. As Buddha noted:

All human unhappiness comes from not facing reality squarely, exactly as it is.

The desire for enlightenment creates a lot of angst and misery in people, particularly when they don't know what enlightenment is or what the process to find it is supposed to produce. Over the past 2,500 years since Buddha found his own way out of the first cognition illusion, his teachings have been corrupted by priests who pose as Masters, but who have not mastered their own egos, or they wouldn't present themselves as authoritative Masters to hold their positions of power. His teachings have been turned into a global institutionalized religion, yet there is nothing in his teachings that remotely endorses such a thing. In fact, the creation of institutional Buddhism is an utter corruption and inversion to what the man taught. Taking his teachings about the suffering of the consciousness and turning that into the base translation of the physically suffering masses tarnishes his name and belittles what he taught. The following passages should clarify once and for all that Buddha was not a religion-maker:

"We are what we think. All that we are arises with our thoughts. With our thoughts, we make the world."

"We are shaped by our thoughts; we become what we think. When the mind is pure, joy follows like a shadow that never leaves."

"It is a man's own mind, not his enemy or foe, that lures him to evil ways."

"The Way is not in the sky; the Way is in the heart."

"Your worst enemy cannot harm you as much as your own unguarded thoughts."

"A man who conquers himself is greater than one who conquers a thousand men in battle."

"The mind is everything. What you think, you become."

"We are what we think. All that we are arises with our thoughts. With our thoughts, we make the world."

"All that we are is the result of what we have thought."

"We are what we think. All that we are arises with our thoughts. With our thoughts, we make our world."

"Peace comes from within. Do not seek it without."

"All wrong-doing arises because of mind. If mind is transformed can wrong-doing remain?"

Given the context and the 'code key' to understanding I have provided herein, then it should be evident that what Buddha taught as the path to enlightenment is one of personal conquest of the illusionary hapiym ego so one can claim their cognitive sovereignty and attain true freedom. This process of overcoming and transcending the world of first cognition perceptions was referred to by don Juan as *'stopping the world'*. In this personal quest, which is the most difficult of undertakings, one must challenge the system of consciousness that rules humanity at this time – the first cognition system of perceptual reality based on false beliefs about the world and false beliefs about ourselves which the ego has convinced us is reality. To step into the second cognition, we must remove these illusions and, as Buddha noted, 'face reality squarely, exactly as it is,' not how we want to *believe* it is. In a world built on perceptual beliefs, then there is no reality of value to be found, only beliefs founded on hope and fear and the wish that what we believe is true.

What he means when he says that we are shaped by our thoughts is that, whatever you embrace as a belief, whether of the external world or your own inner psyche, we are controlled by those thoughts, and those thoughts dictate our perception of reality. If your thoughts are locked into a false perceptual reality, filled with anxiety and fear, then that is the reality in which you will live. This is the suffering of which Buddha taught, the suffering of consciousness ruled by the false ego. When you can transcend this false perception of reality and discover who you really are underneath all the self-deceit created in your mind by the false ego through the process of letting go of all those illusionary beliefs, then you will find a peace of mind, a stillness from the chaotic thoughts of the false ego that never shuts up in your own mind. When you kill the false ego, this world of cognitive peace descends of its own accord and you will lose all the fears that now control you living in this first cognition world of false perceptions and false beliefs about oneself.

This stillness of the mind and silencing the voice of the false ego, what don Juan called the 'inner dialogue', is what leads to that higher state of cognitive awareness. What Buddha taught in his manner for the people of his time, don Juan taught in his manner to later generations. Jesus taught the same principles through parables to the people of his time just as Friedrich Nietzsche sought to teach them to others in his era and ever since, as will be revealed as we progress further in this book.

The problem in explaining these principles about a higher state of human cognitive awareness, is that our present first cognition system of consciousness has no point of relationship through experience with which to comprehend it. It is so foreign to our way of thinking that it can only sound mystical. When, over the millennia, these teachings have been corrupted by religion-makers whose only agenda was to control humanity, then the true nature of these truths gets even further removed from our understanding. We find ourselves misdirected onto paths with an ulterior motive other than the presentation of truth. These truths have become obscured and distant, intentionally overlaid with religious myths and lies to fulfill a darker agenda of control, to confuse the teachings, and further keep them out of our reach. Trying to understand them from the corrupted context from which they have been delivered to us by institutionalized religious thinking and mystical mythology is why they have not been understood in full to this day.

The false self that Buddha referred to in his teachings, don Juan instructed Castenada was his 'person', and that Castenada's person had to die before he could become a true spirit warrior, or sorcerer, using don Juan's terminology. The language and how the concept was presented may be different, but the ultimate core meaning is exactly the same. Before one can free their consciousness, one must kill off this false ego 'person' before they can step into and realize truth and discover who they really are beneath these perceptual lies we have been forced to embrace about ourselves at the manipulation of the hapiym virus. It matters not whether one is called a sorcerer, the Buddha, or the Christ, they are all concepts that presented the same ideas about the advancement of humanity into something greater than it presently is or can imagine. To accomplish this feat of ego destruction from which an individual can launch themselves into the second cognition requires, above all, coming face to face with the lies we embrace about our perceptual reality and the lies we embrace about ourselves. To attain this second cognition state of being requires a form of psychological house cleaning. There is nothing mystical in this process, it is simply gut-wrenching, hard, emotional psychological work that one must face and accomplish to reach that state of second cognition awareness. As Buddha noted:

> *"The fault of others is easily perceived, but that of oneself is difficult to perceive; a man winnows his neighbor's faults like chaff, but his own fault he hides, as a cheat hides the bad die from the gambler."*

The false ego is quick to blame and find fault in others, but it will never look at itself as the cause of its own cognitive suffering. The hapiym virus will cast aspersions of its own faults onto others rather than take ownership of its own shortcomings. In the field of Psychology, this practice is called projecting. Before Psychology even existed as a professional trade, the leaders who taught about cognitive advancement saw this failure with the false ego. By comparison, Jesus taught:

> *"Why do you look at the speck that is in your brother's eye, but do not notice the log that is in your own eye?" Matt 7:3*

"You hypocrite! First take the beam out of your own eye, and then you will see clearly to remove the speck from your brother's eye." Matt 7:5

"How can you say, 'Brother, let me take the speck out of your eye,' while you yourself fail to see the beam in your own eye? You hypocrite, first take the beam out of your own eye, and then you will see clearly to remove the speck from your brother's eye." Luke 6:42

"You therefore have no excuse, you who pass judgment on another. For on whatever grounds you judge the other, you are condemning yourself, because you who pass judgment do the same things." Romans 2:1

The last saying from Romans describes psychological projecting of one's faults onto another in an absolute clear fashion that leaves no room for any other interpretation. These sayings of Jesus, a variant on the same theme, are no different than what Buddha taught above. None of these passages refer to anything religious, mystical or holy, they refer to a state of psychological ego behavior that needs to be challenged and overcome, nothing more and nothing less. Therefore, they are teachings about consciousness and the mind, *not religion.*

One must go through a long and burdensome process of digging out all these psychological behavioral programs indoctrinated into us since we were children, face them, and let them go. This is the only way to remove yourself from the quicksand environment of the first cognition system of awareness. Buddha alluded to this cognitive house cleaning this way:

"When you dig a well, there's no sign of water until you reach it, only rocks and dirt to move out of the way. You have removed enough; soon the pure water will flow."

In this parable, the water is the hidden real you buried within, and the rocks and dirt that are in the way preventing you from seeing that you within are all the overlaid illusions of the world and the illusions about yourself. Until the dirt and rocks are moved away in sufficient quantity, you can't see the water, the real you, until this cognitive detritus is removed. Again, although presented in the form of a parable, there is no riddle of meaning here when we approach this saying using the code key I have provided for understanding these teachings. It is a clear allusion to cognitive advancement and is nothing mystical whatsoever.

Buddha was well aware of the process of cognitive clearing, He knew that each of his pupils would have to go through the same process to reach the state of Nirvana that he did. He was fully cognizant of the pitfalls that anyone on that journey encountered as they went through their own destruction of the false self and its world of *maya*. He taught:

"Know well what leads you forward and what holds you back, and choose the path that leads to wisdom."

"There are only two mistakes one can make along the road to truth; not going all the way, and not starting."

"To conquer oneself is a greater task than conquering others"

"Work out your own salvation. Do not depend on others."

"The darkest night is ignorance"

What should be noted is that many presumed Buddhist Masters have violated Buddha's warning about only going part of the way on the path. There are different stages of the progression to second cognition awareness, and many of these stages of development can lead to a state of partial clarity. This level of clarity can still be a trap for the ego, through which the ego deceives one into believing that they have 'arrived' at the presumed destination for cognitive advancement. It is at this dangerous stage of development where the ego once again deceives the individual, and this clarity has turned many into so-called gurus or Masters, when they have in fact only achieved partial self-mastery at best, and only journeyed part of the way through the process. Don Juan warned that this type of clarity is the second greatest enemy of one on the path of becoming a spirit warrior. Buddha also saw this type of clarity as an inherent threat on the path to Nirvana, or else he wouldn't have warned against only going part of the way.

When we have our objective defined with clear instructions for what we are seeking to achieve, then our path becomes clear. We know what will move us forward and what will drag us back into the clutches and habits of the virus ego. Unfortunately, with the thousands of years since Buddha lived, the true meaning of his teachings has almost been lost to the realm of religious philosophy and speculation. At the time he lived, he reached many people with his teachings, so many in fact that the dominant Hindu religion of the time issued an edict that 'all Buddhists must be killed'. The measure of Buddha's success is the fact that his teachings spread far enough that they became a threat to the Hindu priestly establishment. His teachings reached the far corners of the Earth spreading Eastward into China and Japan and as far West as the Middle East and Greece by the time of Jesus. Buddhist thought influenced certain Greek philosophers and some of his teachings are paralleled in some of the saying of Jesus 500 years later. Despite the mythology surrounding Buddha, he never felt he was a deity, and he would be appalled at how his teachings have been corrupted and how his person has been religionized, almost deified, by first cognition religious teachers who can only utter philosophy, lacking the understanding of his great wisdom. It was not until the presentation of this book that the record can finally be set straight and his work vindicated in the eyes of the world.

Buddha was only a man, just as Jesus, don Juan, Friedrich Nietzsche, and I am only a man. None were 'holy' individuals in the religious sense. Without understanding that what they did was to remove the false ego and elevate their consciousness to a higher state of cognitive awareness, a feat that anyone who is determined enough can accomplish with diligence, focus, stamina and hard work, they only appear as some kind of foreign creature, a divinity, a holy man, a shaman or philosopher perhaps, to those who have no knowledge of what they tried to teach. The wisdom that comes with reaching the state of second cognition awareness is so foreign to first cognition thinking, where dependence on authority rules the world, that it is incomprehensible within that level of cognitive illusionary awareness.

In a world ruled by excessive and reactive emotional interplay, one who has advanced to a state of emotional balance by growing out of the first cognition world of the hapiym ego, will appear to be an aberration within that world, for they do not over-react emotionally like everyone else in the first cognition world. This is the state of inner peace alluded to by Buddha. One who attains this peace and balance has not lost their emotions, they are simply not ruled by them. This is not a case of repressing one's emotions, but one of ridding themselves of the issues that create reactive emotional responses. By removing the psychological 'triggers' that create these emotional reactions, the emotions come into balance on their own, A couple of sayings by Buddha should clarify this focus on reactive emotions being part of the first cognition world of *maya*:

> *"Emotion arise from Desire, hence an Illusion."*

> *"There is nothing more dreadful than the habit of doubt. Doubt separates people. It is a poison that disintegrates friendships and breaks up pleasant relations. It is a thorn that irritates and hurts; it is a sword that kills."*

> *"Holding on to anger is like grasping a hot coal with the intent of throwing it at someone else; you are the one who gets burned."*

> *"Resolutely train yourself to attain peace."*

If this state of cognitive awareness could not be achieved by man, then why did these forerunners into the second cognition try to teach these principles to mankind? In the case of Jesus, particularly, he was turned into the son of God, a walking god-man, by the priestly establishment which wanted his teachings removed from the masses by making them exclusive to a god-being, and therefore unattainable and incomprehensible except to a God. The damage done to his teachings by religionizing them is unforgivably corrupt and has removed the understanding of them from billions of people over the last 2,000 years. These teachings are for the common man, they always have been, for what they can bring humanity as a form of cognitive evolution is out of no one's reach if they desire that change and growth for themselves. These teachings are not exclusionary, reserved only to shamans or holy men. They are usable by anyone with the focus and desire to use them and do the hard work required to achieve this goal. Second cognition awareness is not reserved for the gods, it is humanity's birthright if it will only reach out and claim it.

What Buddha taught as the illusion of *maya*, Jesus referred as the Devil or the works of the Devil. Nietzsche called it the ego, and don Juan called it the world of the *tonal*. When we can understand that these allusions were only devices or descriptions used to express the same limited state of cognitive awareness called the first cognition, then all of their teachings harmonize without having to bend or twist anything into place. Whether it's *maya*, the Devil, the ego, the 'person', the *tonal* or the first cognition, they all express the same principle from the hands of different teachers using their own tools and methods that lead to the same place – the freedom of second cognition awareness, the kingdom of Heaven, Nirvana, the overman or the *nagual*. The only thing that differs is the manner in which these individuals taught according to their cultural milieus and their personal styles to help those they taught to understand the concepts they presented the best. They taught for the language of their times, and this different manner of teaching methods was referred to by don Juan as the *'tonal of the times'*.

Each generation of humanity differs from its predecessors as man's quest for knowledge continues. As such, these messages about achieving a higher state of human cognitive awareness must also be tailored for the generations to which they are presented for the audience to gain the best understanding of the teachings. How the message may be presented will vary, but the core message and the process required to attain that higher level state of human awareness has not.

In modern times, the false mysticism presented in Christianity, and make no mistake, Christianity is a mystical religion, is being replaced by the new mystical religion of New Age thinking. The New Age Movement has folded in the elements of corrupted mystical Buddhism, philosophical Hinduism, Gnostic Christianity, some mystical Sufism, the occult, and heavy doses of Theosophy, Anthroposophy and UFOism. The New Age is the new mystical religion launched in earnest during the 1960's sex, drug and rock & roll era by Esalen Institute in Big, Sur, California. Esalen sponsored speaking engagements for many of the forerunners of the 'mystical experience by drug use' crowd, such as Timothy Leary, Aldous Huxley, and yes, Carlos Castenada, with his tales of psychedelic drug use to reach altered states of awareness. I have covered this aspect in my other works and will not cover them again here in any more depth than this.

Regardless of Castenada's never understanding the teachings of don Juan himself, his magical tales of drugs and adventure brought don Juan's teachings to the world. The major problem is that people focused on the drugs and the mystical adventures more than the pragmatic teachings offered by don Juan. To this day millions are still seeking understanding for what don Juan taught, but until they have developed the keen discernment required to separate the fictional mystical drug-filled fantasies presented by Castenada from the true teachings of don Juan, they will not reach this understanding of don Juan's teachings. The import and validity of his teachings still awaits the proper attention they deserve. Maybe this book will bring about that long overdue analysis of his work when compared to the other teachers presented in this book.

One other point that needs to be clarified in these teachings before moving forward is the use of the word evil, or sometimes sin. Aside from the moralistic overtones of what these concepts mean to religious adherents, or the general consensus perceptions about good and evil, the evil these teachers refer to is the evil of the ego mind. The sin often referred to in the teachings of Jesus is the sin against consciousness by the ego, not fictionalized concepts of sin devised by priests as a means of controlling morality. You see, it's all a matter of *perception*. This endorses what Buddha taught about what you think being what you are. When your perceptions are governed by specific programs to control your viewpoint, and you can't transcend these indoctrinated perceptions, then you remain a slave to the system that plugged them into your consciousness. The greatest hindrance for anyone on the path to enlightenment is the refusal to expand beyond our ingrained cultural perceptions, to transcend *maya*.

3. THE GALILEAN AND HIS TEACHINGS

Now we will turn to the man they called Jesus and do an analysis of his teachings in this new light and see what they can show us. This is not going to be a rehash of the Bible, the myths about Jesus' youth or anything about him that has been religionized by the Roman Church and passed down to other Protestant variants of that religion. We view Jesus strictly as a man who had attained a higher state of cognitive awareness who tried to teach others how to do the same thing he did. Where Buddha used the term Nirvana, Jesus used the language of his time to tell about the kingdom of Heaven. This is most clearly elucidated from one of the sayings from the *Gospel of Thomas*, one of those texts that didn't make the cut to be included in the biblical Canons at the Council of Nicea where the Bible was *voted* into existence. Within the *Gospel of Thomas*, Jesus said:

> *"If those who lead you say to you, 'See, the kingdom is in the sky,' then the birds of the sky will precede you. If they say to you, 'It is in the sea,' then the fish will precede you. Rather, the kingdom is inside of you, and it is outside of you. When you*

*come to know yourselves, then you will become
known, and you will realize that it is you who are
the sons of the living father. But if you will not
know yourselves, you dwell in poverty and it is you
who are that poverty."*

Given the code key of understanding that I have provided, this passage should become totally unambiguous in its meaning. The kingdom of Heaven is that state of cognitive awareness that comes from transcending first cognition ego awareness. This ego awareness is the poverty of which he is speaking; not physical poverty, but cognitive poverty. He is telling his students that so long as you continue to embrace that system of consciousness, you are living in poverty, and by continuing to feed that system of poverty with your illusionary beliefs, you *are* that poverty.

In John 18:36, Jesus once again describes this kingdom this way:

*"My kingdom is not of this world: if my
kingdom were of this world, then would my
servants fight, that I should not be delivered to the
Jews: but now is my kingdom not from here."*

To fully comprehend the meaning of this passage, one must understand the difference between first cognition consciousness and second cognition consciousness as being two different 'worlds' of perception. The word 'world' is an allusion that has been interpreted literally. When Jesus relates that his kingdom is "not of this world", he doesn't mean planet Earth, he means the world of the first cognition. The first cognition misinterpretation of the true meaning of this statement in a literal sense has wrought a dependency on the idea that Heaven is someplace mystical and otherworldly, and that misperception has deceived billions of people over the millennia into believing in an otherworldly afterlife in a false heaven, never realizing they can live profoundly better lives as human beings in this life when the find the heaven within.

At the time the Bible was being composed, there were many contributors from many lands around the Mediterranean region who contributed to creating them. Everything attributed to being what Jesus said was not necessarily anything he ever uttered. Just as there were many contributing authors to the Dead Sea Scrolls, which I assert were being composed the same time that the Gospels and the New Testament was being written, the Nag Hammadi Library collection of Gnostic texts were a collaboration of the same nature. Before the Bible was finally Canonized in its final form, it had been a work in progress, with many different schools of thought vying for supremacy of their own doctrines within the Canons. Those that lost out in this competition were later deemed heretics and eliminated by the Roman Church.

Every one of these different factions used Jesus as the support pole for their own doctrinal circus tents, and that being the case, many erroneous sayings were attributed to him that were not part of his teachings. Unfortunately, for humanity at large, there has been more myth-making and storytelling about him than those about Buddha, so his true teachings become even more obscure. Only one who has succeeded in reaching the second cognition state of awareness has developed the discernment to separate the wheat from the chaff where his true teachings are concerned. I am going to do my best to offer enough of those examples so the reader and later researchers can learn to discern the true teachings from the false doctrinal overlays and misconceptions of others who never met the man or heard what he taught.

In a close comparison to what Buddha taught, from the *Gospel of Thomas*:

> *"Jesus said, "Let him who seeks continue seeking until he finds. When he finds, he will become troubled. When he becomes troubled, he will be astonished, and he will rule over the All.""*

This passage accurately describes the road to the second cognition. One must continue to find answers to erode all their cognitive beliefs. If they are diligent in this process, they are going to become troubled with what they discover about the lies they have accepted as truth and those bouts of cognitive dissonance about which I reported in the last chapter are going to be part of this progression of seeking. When one can transcend their ego consciousness by admitting and overcoming the perceptual lies they embrace, they will be astonished at the level cognitive tyranny that they have not only been subjected to, but have willingly and unwittingly participated in all their lives. When one reaches the second cognition awareness, or Jesus' Heaven, then they will rule over the 'All', which is themselves.

Probably one of the most confusing sayings attributed to Jesus in the *Gospel of Thomas* is this one:

"When you see one who was not born of woman, prostrate yourselves on your faces and worship him. That one is your father."

When reading any of these sayings, one must always remember that they are allegorical. One of the terms Jesus used to describe transcending into the second cognition awareness is that of being 'born again'. All too many Christians have interpreted being born again as a rite of passage and a testimony of their beliefs, usually occurring with the ritual of immersion baptism. But the term born again meant by Jesus was that of being born again into a new form of conscious awareness. It is only viewed in this context that this saying reveals its true meaning.

Although Jesus no more wanted to be worshipped and revered any more than Buddha did, the driving point of this saying is geared toward understanding that one who has transcended the world of the first cognition creates themselves through their years of transcending that perceptual world. When they succeed in this process, they are thus 'born again' into a new form of consciousness, and are therefore 'not born of woman'. The allegory about prostrating oneself in this passage is an allusion to recognizing one who possesses higher level awareness, and the allusion to the father is about recognizing who can lead you to understand these things. They are not to be taken literally in regard to worshipping anyone.

One of the most misunderstood of his messages is found both in the *Gospel of Thomas* as well as in Matthew 10:34 & 35 where he says:

> *"Men think, perhaps, that it is peace which I have come to cast upon the world. They do not know that it is dissension which I have come to cast upon the earth: fire, sword, and war. For there will be five in a house: three will be against two, and two against three, the father against the son, and the son against the father. And they will stand solitary."* – *Gospel of Thomas*

> *"Think not that I am come to send peace on earth: I came not to send peace, but a sword."* - *Matt. 10:34*

> *"For I am come to set a man at variance against his father, and the daughter against her mother, and the daughter-in-law against her mother-in-law."* - *Matt 10:35*

To this very day, Christian scholars still don't understand the meaning of these passages. These words make no sense in the overlaid religious concept of Jesus as the Prince of Peace myth fabricated from the Pauline adaptation and corruption of his teachings, but if you look at the opposition created between first and second cognition humans, then you fully understand what these words mean about dividing households based on his teachings. The message becomes poignantly clear. Many readers may have seen or experienced the conflict offered from the first cognition world to second cognition path teachings as you seek your own path to enlightenment, some of you even under your own roofs. Such resistive actions fully reflect what Jesus related in these sayings. He was fully aware that his teachings would create friction between the rigid first cognition egos, steeped in their traditions, religions and cultures, and people choosing to embrace second cognition teachings and seeing the lies of the first cognition world and sharing the truth with people. He knew that there would be conflict even in families if one chose the path to advancement and the other family members chose to remain unchanging and ruled by their ego. The sword has nothing to do with steel and violence in a literal sense, but is an allegory for the battle between truth and the lies.

The dissension he relates in the *Gospel of Thomas* passage is the dissension that results when rigid first cognition thinking and belief is faced with ideas that challenge one's perception of reality. Within the world of the first cognition, preservation of the status quo is paramount in people's minds. They do not want to admit that their perceptions and beliefs might remotely be in error, so the general historical response has always been to kill the messenger, just as they nailed Jesus to the cross. Such advanced ideas are a threat in a world where everything is spelled out for us, where our traditions, cultures, religious and political beliefs shape our perception of reality and define who we think we are. Protecting this cognitive turf becomes an imperative, and any threat to that cognitive turf is deemed an enemy which must be dealt with. It is not the advanced human being who will bring this war, but those who refuse not only to change, but are threatened by foreign ideas, who must silence the voice of dissent.

This is exactly what happened to Friedrich Nietzsche when he declared that 'God is Dead'. He was blackballed and prevented from pursuing his livelihood, and he could find no place to get his works published for wider distribution. This is how the first cognition world kills any ideas that challenge its perceptual mass superiority. It's not enough to find an idea challenging and just mind your own business about it, such ideas must be eliminated before they can infect others and disrupt the false peace of the herd living with its status quo perceptions. This is the nature of the virus-infected human mind in the first cognition. It is disdainfully predictable in this regard, and it has not changed one whit from the time Jesus walked the Earth until now. The first cognition mindset is rigid and ossified. As don Juan noted about the predator's mind, it is "baroque, contradictory, morose and filled with fear". This fully describes the rigidity of first cognition consciousness. It is this inherent fear that we may be *wrong* that rules our psyches and keeps us unwilling to face the truth, which keeps our consciousness ever stagnant and unmoving, never evolving into what we can become as a species. It is this inherent fear of change that demands that we kill the messenger who makes us uncomfortable and disrupts our false ego perceptions. This is the root of the dissension that Jesus taught about, and it is still alive and as unchanging in the human psyche today as it was 2,000 years ago.

In the old *X-Files* TV series, the tag line was "The Truth is Out There". In the context of cognitive advancement, the truth is still out there for those who have the drive and desire to find it. One may have to dig a bit to unearth it, but the truth is there awaiting discovery by the most diligent of seekers. As Jesus taught:

"Recognize what is in your sight, and that which is hidden from you will become plain to you. For there is nothing hidden which will not become manifest." – Gospel of Thomas

For there is nothing hidden that will not be revealed, and nothing concealed that will not be known and illuminated. – Luke 8:17 - Berean Study Bible version

"And I say unto you, Ask, and it shall be given you; seek, and ye shall find; knock, and it shall be opened unto you" – Luke 11:9 - KJV.

"He who seeks will find, and he who knocks will be let in." – Gospel of Thomas

Along these same lines, Buddha taught:

"Three things cannot be long hidden: the sun, the moon, and the truth."

Each of these sayings are relevant to one seeking enlightenment. The door to Nirvana, Heaven or the second cognition is not going to open itself for anyone who does not do so on their own. If one doesn't actively seek to find the truth, to discover what lays hidden from their perception because they are not motivated to find it, they will never find it. The teachings have nothing to do with a dependency on God, nor do these sayings remotely intimate that kind of dependency. This is all about the individual path to cognitive advancement. These sayings are statements on what one must do if they intend to find what they are seeking. It requires personal effort and fortitude to not only find the truth, but to face the truth and accept it, especially if that truth flies in the face of what you would prefer to believe. Truth will overshadow beliefs at every turn if one but allows it and accepts it. Denying truth because it doesn't fit in with one's own cognitive biases will only leave you wanting in the end.

This is a solitary path made for the individual who is willing to evolve their own consciousness. That individual will always swim against the current of the first cognition status quo. Even Jesus noted this with sayings from the *Gospel of Thomas*:

"Show me the stone which the builders have rejected. That one is the cornerstone."

"Blessed are you when you are hated and persecuted. Wherever you have been persecuted they will find no place."

"Blessed are they who have been persecuted within themselves. It is they who have truly come to know the father. Blessed are the hungry, for the belly of him who desires will be filled."

"Many are standing at the door, but it is the solitary who will enter the bridal chamber."

"He who is near me is near the fire, and he who is far from me is far from the kingdom."

When viewed in the context of teachings about advancing one's consciousness, these sayings take on a meaning as yet unperceived by most people. The builders in the first saying are representative of the first cognition world in general, and the stone they reject is the solitary individual who seeks to break away from that system of consciousness as the cornerstone upon which to build a new world. The sayings about being persecuted should be self-evident given what I have already shared above. The allegory about those persecuted within themselves is another allusion to the cognitive dissonance and psychological turmoil that comes with this process.

One of the most poignant sayings in regard to the first cognition world from the *Gospel of Thomas* is:

> *"I took my place in the midst of the world, and I appeared to them in flesh. I found all of them intoxicated; I found none of them thirsty. And my soul became afflicted for the sons of men, because they are blind in their hearts and do not have sight; for empty they came into the world, and empty too they seek to leave the world. But for the moment they are intoxicated. When they shake off their wine, then they will repent."*

The intoxication alluded to in this allegory is the seduction of the first cognition system of ego awareness. To my knowledge, this saying didn't pass muster to make it into the Canonized New Testament. The saying refers to the fact that those immersed in that system of consciousness are not even thirsty enough to desire anything more than what is known, they are intoxicated with the cognitive illusion. If one decides to shake off the intoxicating lures of that system of ego consciousness, then they can grow, if not, they will live and die in that system never knowing something better exists. Within that system of ego awareness, all are walking around blind from the truth, and Jesus had this to say about that in a saying from the *Gospel of Thomas*:

> *"If a blind man leads a blind man, they will both fall into a pit."*

This saying did make it into the Bible in Matthew 15:14:

"Disregard them! They are blind guides. If a blind man leads a blind man, both will fall into a pit."

The blind guides are the authoritative teachers of the first cognition world, whether they are secular or religious (spiritual). When following teachers blindly in this fashion, then both the guide and the follower meet cognitive misfortune (fall into a ditch), for neither of them are qualified to reveal the truth and both will fall into error thinking that their system of perception is the correct one to follow.

It is not my chosen task to explain each and every one of the sayings attributed to Jesus. This is not necessary given the context of how to translate what they mean. With these new insights in hand, then the randomly selected verses to follow should reveal their meaning. These parables are all in the New Testament Gospels. The following is Jesus' explanation on the meaning of the parable of the tares:

"He that soweth the good seed is the Son of man; the field is the world; the good seed are the children of the kingdom; but the tares are the children of the wicked one; the enemy that sowed them is the devil; the harvest is the end of the world; and the reapers are the angels."

"As therefore the tares are gathered and burned in the fire; so shall it be in the end of this world. The Son of man shall send forth his angels, and they shall gather out of his kingdom all things that offend, and them which do iniquity; and shall cast them into a furnace of fire: there shall be wailing and gnashing of teeth.

Then shall the righteous shine forth as the sun in the kingdom of their Father.

Who hath ears to hear, let him hear."

"Whereunto shall we liken the kingdom of God? or with what comparison shall we compare it? A grain of mustard seed is the least of all seeds: is indeed less than all the seeds that be in the earth; but when it is sown in the earth, it groweth up: it becometh greater than all herbs; it shooteth out great branches, and becometh a tree, so that the fowls of the air come and lodge in the branches thereof."

"Verily, verily, I say unto thee, Except a man be born again, he cannot see the kingdom of God."

"If I have told you earthly things, and ye believe not, how shall ye believe, if I tell you of

heavenly things? And no man hath ascended up to heaven, but he that came down from heaven, even the Son of man which is in heaven."

"I have meat to eat that ye know not of."

"Except ye see signs and wonders, ye will not believe."

"Verily, verily, I say unto you. The hour is coming, and now is, when the dead shall hear the voice of the Son of God: and they that hear shall live. For as the Father hath life in himself; so hath he given to the Son to have life in himself; and hath given him authority to execute judgment also because he is the Son of man. Marvel not at this: for the hour is coming, in the which all that are in the graves shall hear his voice, and shall come forth; they that have done good, unto the resurrection of life; and they that have done evil, unto the resurrection of damnation."

As noted earlier, all of these sayings must be interpreted in the light of cognitive advancement, not a religious context. When Jesus speaks about those that are in their graves, he is not talking about corpses, but those who live in the grave of the ego's perceptual reality. This is the meaning of one of his other sayings about 'Leaving the dead to bury the dead'. All of these sayings are allegorical but have been taken to be literal religious truth to produce a fear of judgment and damnation by priests who would subjugate humanity and human consciousness. The resurrection of life is not immortality or life after death, but represents finding freedom from the first cognition ego prison for our consciousness. This 'resurrection' is being born again into the higher cognitive 'heaven' as a human on Earth, not some mystical heaven above.

The 'end of the world' foretold in these parables is not the destruction of the Earth as so many Christians in the religious ego depravity of their faith actually believe and pray for, but portend and end of the world of the ego, the first cognition illusion, which *will* create the despair and gnashing of teeth as that cognitive world is destroyed and its false beliefs cast into the fire

To understand other parables, one must move past the concept of God as the Father, and view the Father as an allusion for higher consciousness. This becomes evident when Jesus refers to his 'Father's Kingdom' in other passages, or doing his Father's work by teaching his 'gospel'. We must always keep in mind that he was speaking the language and to the consciousness of the people of his time in terms they could best understand through his parables and allegories. We have no touchstone in our present era to comprehend any of that because we did not live then to fully understand his cultural milieu except through secondhand reporting. We can't cast our modern perceptions backwards and make them fit into that world and think we have any understanding of it.

"But I have greater witness than that of John: for the works which the Father hath given me to finish, the same works that I do, bear witness of me, that the Father hath sent me. And the Father himself, which hath sent me, hath borne witness of me. Ye have neither heard his voice at any time, nor seen his shape. And ye have not his word abiding in you: for whom he hath sent, him ye believe not."

"I receive not honor from men. But I know you, that ye have not the love of God in you. I am come in my Father's name, and ye receive me not: if another shall come in his own name, him ye will receive. How can ye believe, which receive honor one of another, and seek not the honor that cometh from God only?"

This last passage, once again, is a chastisement for those who will listen to the voice of first cognition authorities, "which receive honor one from another", but who will not listen to anyone who is not an authority figure because of that lack of first cognition perceptions of authority, whether that is academic, political, religious or otherwise. This is a major failing of living in and embracing the first cognition system of ego awareness, and that is the dependence on authority syndrome. This saying couples with the blind leading the blind saying above.

"The Spirit of the Lord is upon me, because he hath anointed me to preach the gospel to the poor; he hath sent me to heal the brokenhearted, to preach deliverance to the captives, and recovering of sight to the blind, to set at liberty them that are bruised, to preach the acceptable year of the Lord."

The healing that Jesus is referring to in this passage, and others where he 'healed the blind' have nothing to do with the physical infirmity of blindness, but are about removing the cognitive blinders from people's eyes by teaching them the truth of the reality they do not see. To heal the brokenhearted is a form of cognitive emotional healing of the ego psyche, and the deliverance of captives is a reference to all those held in bondage in the ego realm of deception and illusion. His teachings, as with ours, and the other men referenced in this volume, are designed to provide liberty to the cognitively bruised. So, all the references to his 'miraculous' healing abilities have a more pragmatic application when viewed in light of cognitive healing rather than the miraculous healing of physical infirmities. Once again, allegory is exchanged for literalism and Jesus the man becomes a 'one of a kind' miracle worker, a god-man.

Jesus, like Buddha, drew crowds of followers wherever he went. The Sermon on the Mount is filled with allegories about his 'kingdom of Heaven' for those with ears to hear and understand his messages:

Blessed are the poor in spirit: for theirs is the kingdom of heaven.

Blessed are they that mourn: for they shall be comforted.

Blessed are the meek: for they shall inherit the earth.

Blessed are they which do hunger and thirst after righteousness: for they shall be filled.

Blessed are the merciful: for they shall obtain mercy.

Blessed are the pure in heart: for they shall see God.

Blessed are the peacemakers: for they shall be called the children of God.

Blessed are they which are persecuted for righteousness' sake: for theirs is the kingdom of heaven.

Blessed are ye, when men shall revile you, and persecute you, and shall say all manner of evil against you falsely, for my sake.

Rejoice, and be exceeding glad: for great is your reward in heaven: for so persecuted they the prophets which were before you.

Can you see the meaning of these teachings now when presented in this new light? Do you find understanding in his promises from this sermon? Get past the God dependency of belief and step into the truth of what is. Read the God of Jesus' teachings as an allegory, not a literal supernatural entity as religionists have interpreted throughout the ages. Read his use of 'righteousness' as no different than Buddha's 'right mind', not in the sense of otherworldly religious ego supremacy as a doctrinaire of organized Christianity. Each individual who can transition their consciousness into the second cognition awareness becomes another guide to others. As Jesus instructed:

"Ye are the light of the world. A city that is set on a hill cannot be hid. Neither do men light a candle, and put it under a bushel, but on a candlestick; and it giveth light unto all that are in the house. Let your light so shine before men, that they may see your good works, and glorify your Father which is in heaven."

"And if thy right eye offend thee, pluck it out, and cast it from thee: for it is profitable for thee that one of thy members should perish, and not that thy whole body should be cast into hell.

And if thy right hand offend thee, cut it off, and cast it from thee, for it is profitable for thee that one of thy members should perish, and not that thy whole body should be cast into hell."

This last allegory is noteworthy of explanation because it, too, has been greatly misunderstood over the centuries. In this saying Jesus is not talking about literal body parts, but is in fact talking about beliefs and ideas and how they should be rejected, which is what the offending body parts in the allegory represent, in order to save the whole of your consciousness. By rejecting the *beliefs* we find offensive, particularly the beliefs we have embraced about our ego self and would rather embrace than let go of, we save our full consciousness by excising the offending and incorrect beliefs. The journey to Nirvana requires deep and critical self-examination. We must all come face to face with ourselves and excise all the beliefs and habits the ego self has lied to us about and made us believe. Confronting and letting go of these self-deceptions is the hardest thing you will ever do, but it is a requirement for advancing oneself into cognitive freedom. This parable is a reflection of this mandate for cognitive growth.

> *"And when thou prayest, thou shalt not be as the hyprocites are: for they love to pray standing in the synagogues and in the corners of the streets, that they may be seen of men. Verily I say unto you, They have their reward. But thou, when thou prayest, enter into thy closet, and when thou hast shut thy door, pray to thy Father which is in secret; and thy Father which seeth in secret shall reward thee openly.*
>
> *But when ye pray, use not vain repetitions, as the heathen do: for they think that they shall be heard for their much speaking. Be not ye therefore like unto them: for your Father knoweth what things ye have need of, before ye ask him."*

These passages, like many others, have led people to believe that their actions in their churches and their synagogues are earning them some type of reward in the fictional concept of heaven as an otherworldly place. These literal interpretations have led millions of ego-driven believers to commit many acts, not all of them good (Crusades and Jihads for instance), thinking they are pleasing their God. By telling his disciples to do their praying in secret, it is a statement, once again, that this is a personal path and not a group endeavor as religions present to the ego in a group environment. In such cases, the group ego reinforces the individual ego and its beliefs and it is therefore no longer a personal path, but one of ego group solidarity. This doesn't mean that secrecy is exactly what is meant in the literal sense of the word, but that your personal work is yours and yours alone, so it must be done in private since you are doing most of this psychological work to advance yourself in your own mind.

This work is not done for accolades or public acknowledgment as the public praying and other religious displays referred to, such as Hare Krishna's dressing in their robes, dancing and chanting and begging for money, nor the public displays such as those performed by Jews before the wailing wall, or participating in the Hajj in Islam. These are all displays of the hungry ego self, seeking approval in the eyes of their presumed gods and their fellow religionists to show how 'holy' they are. This is no different than group meditations publicly performed by modern spiritual seekers in the New Age arena who are seeking to change the world, using meditation as just another form of public praying hiding behind a different mask.

In the second passage, the treasures referred to are those of consciousness and focusing on the cognitive reality in which one chooses to live. If we choose to embrace the first cognition reality, the reference to evil in this context, then that is all we will see. If we choose to focus on advancing ourselves, as we advance we begin collecting the 'treasures' of truth, which can never be taken from us. Again, this accumulation of treasures is not achieved by public displays of our religious beliefs.

> *"Give not that which is holy unto the dogs,*
> *neither cast ye your pearls before swine, lest they*
> *trample them under their feet, and turn again and*
> *rend you."*

"Ask, and it shall be given you; seek, and ye shall find; knock, and it shall be opened unto you: for every one that asketh receiveth; and he that seeketh findeth; and to him that knocketh it shall be opened.

Or what man is there of you, whom if his son ask bread, will he give him a stone? Or if he asks a fish, will he give him a serpent? If ye then, being evil, know how to give good gifts unto your children, how much more shall your Father which is in heaven give good things to them that ask him?"

"Enter ye in at the strait gate: for wide is the gate, and broad is the way, that leadeth to destruction, and many there be which go in thereat: because strait is the gate, and narrow is the way, which leadeth unto life, and few there be that find it."

"Beware of false prophets, which come to you in sheep's clothing, but inwardly they are ravening wolves. Ye shall know them by their fruits. Do men gather grapes of thorns, or figs of thistles? Even so every good tree bringeth forth good fruit; but a corrupt tree bringeth forth evil fruit. A good tree cannot bring forth evil fruit,

neither can a corrupt tree bring forth good fruit. Every tree that bringeth not forth good fruit is hewn down, and cast into the fire. Wherefore by their fruits ye shall know them."

"Therefore whosoever heareth these sayings of mine, and doeth them, I will liken him unto a wise man, which built his house upon a rock: and the rain descended, and the floods came, and the winds blew, and beat upon that house: and it fell not: for it was founded upon a rock."

"And every one that heareth these sayings of mine, and doeth them not, shall be likened unto a foolish man, which built his house upon the sand: and the rain descended, and the floods came, and the winds blew, and beat upon that house; and it fell: and great was the fall of it."

The parable of the rock has been another teaching that has been abused to create a dependency on Jesus as God, where Christians believe by professing their faith in that dependency on the myth of Jesus, is their house built on rock, but in truth, their ego house is the one built on sand whose illusions cannot stand up to the pressures of the storm of greater consciousness and truth. Again, in the last two passages Jesus is talking about *'doing'* what he does, not believing in what he says. This should not escape your notice. By his assertions, we are again told that these things can be accomplished by anyone to follows the teachings with personal *action*. Don Juan also taught this same principle of 'acting' if one wants to advance. It is our actions that make the doing, and the doing through action that makes growth and willful evolution possible. Without action and doing, nothing happens. One must put their money where their mouth is to succeed on this path to higher level cognitive awareness, and that comes through acting, not trying to wish it into existence for you. Simply believing it will be handed to you because you believe it to be true will always leave you wanting and unmoved.

"They that be whole need not a physician, but they that are sick. But go ye and learn what that meaneth. I will have mercy, and not sacrifice: for I am not come to call the righteous, but sinners to repentance."

"Can the blind lead the blind? shall they not both fall into the ditch? The disciple is not above his master: **but every one that is perfect shall be as his master***."*

"And why call ye me, Lord, Lord, and do not the things which I say? Whosoever cometh to me, **and heareth my sayings, and doeth them***, I will shew you to whom he is like:*

He is like a man which built a house, and digged deep, and laid the foundation on a rock:

and when the flood arose, the stream beat vehemently upon that house, and could not shake it: for it was founded upon a rock. But he that heareth, and doeth not, is like a man that without a foundation built a house upon the earth; against which the stream did beat vehemently, and immediately it fell; and the ruin of that house was great."

*"Go thy way; and **as thou hast believed**, so be it done unto thee."*

"All things are delivered unto me of my Father, and no man knoweth the Son, but the Father; neither knoweth any man the Father, save the Son, and he to whomsoever the Son will reveal him."

[All bold emphasis mine]

This last passage requires clarification for understanding in the context of personal growth. The Son in this verse is the individual self, the true self buried under the ego. No man can know his true self but himself. The Father, once again, is an allusion to one's own internal psoyca sentience. So, what transpires in this passage is that Jesus is stating that no one can know him except himself, and no one can know any other but their own inner self – the Son being known by their own Father. He is saying that only your own true self can reveal itself to you and to no one else. Only you can know who you are and you cannot be told who you really are by another, or let another define to you who you are. Each of us has our own Father of consciousness, our own psoyca, and only the Son who seeks that consciousness will be the one to find it, and no one else.

Here again, Jesus is not teaching a doctrine of dependency to follow him or believe in him, but that one must learn to follow themselves because no one can find your own inner self but you. Only interpreted in this context does this passage have any meaning whatsoever. Although the Christian dependency doctrine may suggest that only through Jesus can you know the Jewish God, this is not what this passage means in its truest context.

When asked by one of his disciples why he taught in parables, Jesus answered:

> *"Because it is given unto you to know the mysteries of the kingdom of heaven, but to them it is not given but in parables: unto them that are without, all these things are done in parables.*
>
> *For whosoever hath, to him shall be given, and he shall have more abundance: but whosoever hath not, from him shall be taken away even that he hath.*
>
> *Therefore speak I to them in parables: because they seeing see not; and hearing they hear not, neither do they understand.*
>
> *And in them is fulfilled the prophecy of Esaias, which saith, By hearing ye shall hear, and*

shall not understand; and seeing ye shall see, and shall not perceive: for this people's heart is waxed gross, and their ears are dull of hearing, and their eyes they have closed; lest at any time they should see with their eyes, and hear with their ears, and should understand with their heart, and should be converted, and I should heal them, and their sins should be forgiven them.

But blessed are your eyes, for they see: and your ears, for they hear. For verily I say unto you, That many prophets and righteous men have desired to see those things which ye see, and have not seen them; and to hear those things which ye hear, and have not heard them."

The revelations contained in the passage clearly sum up the cognitive rigidity of people living in the first cognition. The world is populated with people who choose to live lives of self-enforced selective blindness. They have neither the eyes to see anything more than the world they perceive, nor the ears to listen to anything that disagrees with their perceptions about reality. In the first cognition reality, people's ears have grown dull and they have closed their eyes to anything that goes against the grain of their indoctrinated beliefs and perceptions. Jesus' assessment of the masses of humanity in his time are no different than the consciousness of humanity in the present age. Whether we use allegories or parables, one who refuses to listen cannot hear and one who refuses to try and see remains blind to these teachings.

As Jesus said repeatedly, let those with ears hear. Do you have the ears to finally hear his message and try to understand his teachings in their correct context, or are your ears dull and your eyes closed too?

What is just revealed is why humanity has not advanced its consciousness in the 2,500 years since Buddha introduced these same teachings to humanity. Willful ignorance and willful blindness keeps humanity from evolving into what it can become through the process of willful evolution, which is the only solution to this conundrum. The destiny of humanity is in the hands of humanity itself. If it chooses to travel the same road it always had, willfully deaf and blind, then there will be no advancement of this species. Its consciousness will remain as it always has, repetitive, predictable and manageable by those who know how to keep the masses cowed with promises of supernatural rewards, or by those who know how to herd humanity into their corrals of tyranny through psychological manipulation. The only way to break this cycle is when enough people see the truth of these teachings can transcend their beliefs and accept truth, and it is only by accepting the truth that one will acquire wisdom. When enough people make this willful choice, and decide to advance themselves, only then will we discover what truly being human is, and not until.

"Behold, I send you forth as sheep in the midst of wolves: be ye therefore wise as serpents, and harmless as doves."

*"The disciple is not above his master, nor the servant above his lord. It is enough for the disciple that he be **as** his master, and the servant **as** his lord."*

"He that receiveth you receiveth me, and he that receiveth me receiveth him that sent me. He that receiveth a prophet in the name of a prophet shall receive a prophet's reward; and he that receiveth a righteous man in the name of a righteous man shall receive a righteous man's reward."

"If any man will come after me, whosoever will, let him deny himself, and take up his cross daily, and follow me.

For whosoever will save his life shall lose it: but whosoever will lose his life for my sake and the gospel's, the same shall save it. For what shall it profit a man, what is a man advantaged, if he gain the whole world, and lose himself, lose his own soul? or be cast away? Or what shall a man give in exchange for his soul? For the Son of man shall come in the glory of his Father with his angels; and then he shall reward every man according to his works.

Whosoever therefore shall be ashamed of me and of my words, in this adulterous and sinful

*generation, of him also shall the Son of man be
ashamed, when he shall come in his own glory: and
cometh in the glory of his Father with his holy
angels".*

To understand the full meaning of this passage, where Jesus says that "whosoever shall save his life shall lose it", it does not mean any form of martyrdom in dying for a religion, which is unfortunately how all too many Christians interpreted this teaching. It means that one's ego must die before the true self can be found. As he further elucidates, "but whosoever will lose his life for my sake and the gospel's, the same shall save it", it means that when you lose the illusionary life of the ego, you will find the life of the true inner psoyca self and shall save yourself. What Jesus is relating in this passage is no different than don Juan teaching Castenada that his 'person' must die. Both are allusions to the death of the false ego and the 'salvation' of finding the true self within.

*"I am the light of the world: he that
followeth me shall not walk in darkness, but shall
have the light of life."*

*"Though I bear record of myself, yet my
record is true: for I know whence I came, and
whither I go; but ye cannot tell whence I come, and
whither I go. Ye judge after the flesh; I judge no*

man. And yet if I judge, my judgment is true: for I am not alone, but I and the Father that sent me.

It is also written in your law, that the testimony of two men is true. I am one that bear witness of myself, and the Father that sent me beareth witness of me."

"Ye neither know me, nor my Father: if ye had known me, ye should have known my Father also."

"Ye are from beneath; I am from above: ye are of this world; I am not of this world. I said therefore unto you that ye shall die in your sins: for if ye believe not that I am he, ye shall die in your sins."

This last passage once more elucidates the different 'worlds' of perception presented by the first and second cognition. When one reaches that higher state of cognitive awareness, they can see all the poisons and ills, 'sins', of the first cognition reality. But as Jesus accurately stated that he is not 'of the first cognition world', it has been misconstrued to mean some other kind of supernatural world to first cognition perceptions. The world in which Jesus lived, cognitively speaking, is the world of the second cognition awareness, and it is available to anyone who strives to reach it through hard work and diligence. It is not inaccessible, but it is very difficult to get there. As don Juan taught, reaching that goal is not impossible, but there is a price to be paid to get there. Most are unwilling to pay the entry fee.

"When ye have lifted up the Son of man, then shall ye know that I am he, and that I do nothing of myself; but as my Father hath taught me, I speak these things. And he that sent me is with me: the Father hath not left me alone; for I do always those things that please him."

"If ye continue in my word, then are ye my disciples indeed; and ye shall know the truth, and the truth shall make you free."

"Verily, verily, I say unto you, Whosoever committeth sin is the servant of sin. And the servant abideth not in the house for ever: but the Son abideth ever. If the Son therefore shall make you free, ye shall be free indeed."

In this last passage, the reference to the Son is not to Jesus as most Christians presume, but to the Son who is yourself, your inner psoyca. It is your own internal Son who can make you free and no other, as discussed previously.

I feel that I have presented more than enough of the second cognition teachings of Jesus in this chapter to make my case. The evidence stands clear for those with the ears to hear and the eyes to see these truths. Only those who insist on maintaining their world of illusionary beliefs will deny these teachings, and continue to live, as Jesus said, "in sin". There is no greater sin against consciousness than willful ignorance and the denial used to reinforce that ignorance. Ignorance can be cured, willful ignorance cannot.

4. THE LAST PROPHET – FRIEDRICH NIETZSCHE

"New struggles. -- After Buddha was dead, they still showed his shadow in a cave for centuries -- a colossal, horrible shadow. God is dead, but given the way people are, there may still be caves for millennia in which his shadow is displayed. -- And we -- we must still defeat his shadow as well!"
— Friedrich Nietzsche, The Gay Science

In the first cognition world, humanity has a problem with singularities. By this I mean that humans have been deceived into believing that prophets or teachers only come once and that there can be no other. To Buddhists, Buddha was their singularity. To Christians, Jesus was their singularity. To Muslims, Muhammed was their singularity. The mindset in first cognition awareness that there can be one and only one valid teacher, particularly where the establishment of religions is concerned, blinds humanity in general from seeing the things I am pointing out in this book.

Once one of these singularities is decided upon by the segment of the population that accepts these singularities as singularities, the book is closed and there can be no other. Once this is decided, history and their beliefs become frozen in time. This same mindset about singularities is also present with the concept of monotheism and there only being one God. Although Hinduism is a polytheistic religion, it is still governed by the belief in Brahman, which is the concept of a single overarching consciousness of which humans are only small parts, what Hindus refer to as Atman. In the New Age and modern spiritual arena, this concept of some singular cosmic Oneness or Source as the primary creator of all that is, is also present. In science, they are seeking to prove a Unified Field theory, which is just another case of first cognition singularity thinking. With these valid observations, I think it's safe to say that humanity has a serious cognitive hang-up over singularities.

The problem with the singularity mindset is that it blinds us from seeing a larger picture that may be present just beyond our own cognitive rigidity. In the case of singularity thinking and the acceptance of it, one no longer looks further for alternative answers. This belief in the singularity perception creates a locked-down box to one's perception from which any further investigation is disallowed. When a singularity is found no further questions are allowed, and generally, none sought. It's all been settled. The belief in the singularity is the end of the story where advancing consciousness is concerned because both the story and its ending have been written at the start. The beginning *is* the ending.

If we look at the presentation of history in our classrooms, we are once again faced with singularity thinking, where every facet of history we are taught is merely a snapshot, a moment frozen in time, an event, as much as a painting or photographs are instancea of time frozen to leave an impressionistic legacy to the future. We are taught meaningless names, dates and places that we are instructed to remember that catalogue our history, but these frozen singular instances do not provide us the color of surrounding activities, particularly those of the unwashed masses, which contribute to the snapshot view we call our history. We are only presented with the snapshots of the movers and shakers, those who the elite have deemed worthy of acknowledgments, who are usually from their own ranks. *This* is our history, not the history of the common man or the history of humanity in whole. The common man is hardly a footnote in the histories of this planet. We are only the unwashed masses, the cannon fodder to the never-ceasing wars of the power hungry.

The controlling elite on this planet fear the power of an awakened populace, they always have. This is why they have worked tirelessly to provide bread and circuses, to keep the masses dumb, fat and happy – and let's not forget ignorant – so they can continue to control humanity through such ignorance and fear. We live in a world of spectacle. The news outlets, film and TV media blare the spectacle 24/7, and although we are not observing gladiatorial events and the blood sports of old, we are now mesmerized with new forms of spectacle which draw our attention continually into an illusionary picture painted for us purely to distract us and keep humanity as nothing more than docile slaves to agendas we have no perception about.

The teachings of people like Buddha and Jesus are teachings of personal empowerment. Such teachings were as much a threat to the elite establishment during their lives as the threat that Friedrich Nietzsche presented to the elite of his time. In the cases of Jesus and Buddha, we have stories only partially told. We have teachings that have been sanitized, altered and whitewashed to such a degree with doctrinal overlaying that their meanings are lost to all but those with the keenest eye and the clearest mind. We have instead been told illusionary tales about these teachers being *holy* messengers, and in the case of Jesus, turned him into God walking in flesh, moving his teachings from pragmatic application for the everyman into the realm of supernatural, *godly* unattainment of the principles he taught, i.e. "These are the things of God and let no mere human believe he can attain such wisdom! How dare you think you can be like Jesus!"

Throughout his teachings, Jesus implored his disciples and followers to become like he is by doing the things he did, yet to modern Christians, Jesus was God on Earth and *no one* better even attempt to do the things he did! Jesus is *our* singularity and ours alone! How dare you think you can do the things our god-man did?! Buddha taught the same thing, as did Friedrich Nietzsche, but each of them knew that there would be those who would refuse to listen to their messages - those without ears to hear.

There are hints that what Jesus and Buddha taught was as filled with polemic and vitriol against the superficial illusion that humanity embraced as reality in their times, as much as they challenged the elite institutions of their eras. We see whispers of this in the sanitized teachings when each of these men challenged the ruling priesthoods of their time. When Jesus cautioned his disciples to not cast the pearls of his wisdom teachings before the swine who preferred self-enforced cognitive ignorance, it doesn't get much more graphic and opinionated than that. From this great distance in time, there has been plenty of opportunity to overwrite these messages with false religious doctrines to make the image of these teachers conform to that of the docile holy servant, yet Jesus himself said that he was not here to bring peace, but to bring a sword. These words do not remotely intimate that he was a pushover. I think the same can be said of Buddha. One does not challenge the illusion of the human puppet show without challenging the puppeteers themselves. These men were a threat to the establishment in their time as much as Nietzsche and his polemic was in his time, particularly when he proclaimed, "God is Dead."

One cannot transcend the illusion and not pass scorn on what they see. On can't remain silent in the face of such a massive tyranny over consciousness, especially when one can see a better way to live as a human being. Just as Jesus and Buddha taught the road to personal empowerment, what people call enlightenment, Nietzsche himself walked that same road. The proof of this is found in *Thus Spoke Zarathustra: On the Spirit of Gravity 2,* when he said:

"By many ways, in many ways, I reached
my truth: it was not on one ladder that I climbed to
the height where my eye roams over my distance.

And it was only reluctantly that I ever inquired about the way: that always offended my taste. I preferred to question and try out the ways themselves.

*<u>A trying and questioning was my every move</u>; and verily, one must always learn to answer such questioning. That, however, is **my** taste—not good, not bad, by my taste of which I am no longer ashamed and which I have no wish to hide.*

*<u>"This is **my** way; where is yours?"</u>—thus I answered those who asked me "the way." For **the** way—that does not exist."*

[Bold emphasis in original]

[Underlined emphasis mine]

The human quest for enlightenment, as with all else, is predicated on searching for that singularity, just and Nietzsche noted above by people searching for *"the* way." He is wholly correct in his answer that, *"the* way does not exist." The most relevant question he asks is that same one taught by Jesus and Buddha, "This is *my* way; where is yours?" Do you want to know why every follower of Buddha fails on their own path? The answer is really very simple. They all fail because they are all seeking to walk in Buddha's footsteps and they are not walking in their own! Buddha's path to enlightenment was his and his alone. The same can be said of Jesus, and for Nietzsche. The foregoing passage reveals how this is done, for everyone, in the first paragraph - by "trying and questioning" your "every move". The road that Nietzsche reported that he walked is the same one that every individual seeking their own cognitive freedom must walk. It is the winding and twisting road I had to walk, but it was *my* road, just as each of these men walked their own personal road to the second cognition. Traversing this road, each of these men gained a wisdom that is not available in the first cognition world of illusion. This type of wisdom can't even be *comprehended* when it is explained in detail to your face! To this day our most brilliant and esteemed scholars have not intuited the barest glimmering of what Nietzsche tried to teach mankind where wisdom is concerned.

Just as Nietzsche wrote about having to look into areas that offended him, don Juan taught the same thing, that it is only through looking into what offends us that we learn another perspective. Reading and studying things that only reinforce our beliefs is the path of the lazy man. It's called confirmation bias. It is only through researching the things that we have been told to avoid that the illusion starts to crack and shatter and we begin to grow. This doesn't mean that we have to embrace what we find, but if we continually avoid what makes us psychologically uncomfortable because the ideas conflict with our cultural indoctrination and personal beliefs, then we remain stagnant and unmoving within the illusion. Here again, the singularity rules, with the individual only reinforcing what they want to believe and maintaining that single point of view. It is only through challenging our personal beliefs that we start to unravel the illusion and free our consciousness from it. This is a long and grueling process and there is no quick and easy way to arrive at enlightenment. One thing is for certain, tireless meditation or praying for divine rescue or salvation is not going to take one there.

At the time that Nietzsche wrote his works, the Gnostic texts still laid undiscovered in the Egyptian desert, yet even without such texts as the *Gospel of Thomas* and others, Nietzsche was able to glean enough from the Bible passages to see Jesus' teachings in a more realistic light than any expert theologian or philosopher before him, or since. As Nietzsche noted in *The Antichrist*:

> *"The "kingdom of heaven" is a condition of the heart — not something that comes "over the earth" or "after death." The whole concept of natural death is lacking in the Gospel: death is no bridge, no crossing, it is lacking because it belongs to a completely different, merely apparent, merely useful-as-a-sign world. The "hour of death" is no Christian concept — the "hour," the time, physical life and its crises simply do not exist for the teacher of the "glad tidings"... the "kingdom of God "is not at all what one expects; it has no yesterday and no day after tomorrow, it does not come in a "thousand years" — it is an experience of the heart; it is everywhere, it is nowhere...*

> *This "bringer of glad tidings" died as he had lived, as he had taught— not to "save*

*mankind," but to show how one ought to live. It is
the practice which he bequeathed to mankind..."*

What Nietzsche intuited from the teachings of Jesus is no
different than what is presented in this book. It is a practice of self-
discipline that turns into a way one should live. It is not a
philosophy, and it definitely does not produce a yearning to escape
the life you live in exchange some fictional afterlife or mystical
state of presumed bliss. As Nietzsche further observed in a later
passage from *The Antichrist*:

*"— Only we, we **free-gotten** spirits, have
the prerequisite for understanding something
nineteen centuries have misunderstand — that
instinct and passion become integrity which wages
war on the "holy lie" even more than on any other
lie... They were immeasurably removed from our
loving and careful neutrality, from that cultivation
of the spirit through which alone the divining of
such unfamiliar, such tender things is made
possible: they desired at all times, with a
shameless selfishness, only their own advantage,
they erected the **Church** out of opposition to the
Gospel..."*

[Emphasis in original]

As Nietzsche so capably noted in this passage, it is only
those who have freed their consciousness from the first cognition

ego trap, those ""free-gotten" spirits", who can understand what is contained in these teachings. The muddied waters of the illusion become crystal clear as one transcends the illusion and defeats the ego. Only those who have progressed through this process of self-destruction of the ego and its world of perceptual illusions will win their freedom of consciousness to see these truths for what they are. We see the 'holy lie" in all its permutations, from the Hinduism of old through every mutated religious ideology into today's New Age and modern spiritual beliefs. The beast of the illusion, of dependency, of escapism, of the complete avoidance of personal responsibility to evolve oneself, is present in every religion that promises a mystical form of afterlife, cosmic state of bliss, rescue by aliens, ascending to the 5th dimension, or seeking to better one's chances for the next life in the karmic cycle of reincarnation. It is all the same deceptive beast of the illusion, no matter which garb it wears for each successive generation. This is the great "holy lie" against which every teacher of advanced consciousness has fought.

The lie doesn't change, only the outward doctrinal clothing sold to the masses as their illusionary salve for salvation changes. The teachings of Christ have now morphed into 'Christ Consciousness', Buddha's to 'Buddha Consciousness', under the sway and control of Theosophy morphed into the New Age Movement. The bastardization of the truth with just more mystical hogwash persists as much today as it did during the lifetimes of Buddha and Jesus. The doctrines sold to the humanity are mystically the same, and unfortunately, the consciousness of humanity is equally the same. The 'holy lie' is alive and well in the 21st century.

Nietzsche completes the passage above with this:

> *"If one were to look for signs that behind the great world-game an ironical divinity had control at his fingertips, he would find no small support in the **enormous question mark** called Christianity. That mankind is on its knees in opposition to that which was the origin, the meaning, the **right** of the Gospel, that in the concept "Church" it pronounced holy precisely that which the "bringer of glad tidings" felt to be **beneath him, behind him** — one searches in vain for a greater form of **world-historical irony** ——"*
>
> *[Emphasis in original]*

Nietzsche saw as plainly as I do the detestable inversion of truth that had taken place in the Christianity of his time, which is no different now than it was then, but which is conjoined today with its twin sister, New Ageism. Every doctrine that preaches dependency on some higher source outside ourselves only leads one down the path of cognitive slavery, ever caught in the illusion believing we are lesser beings. By believing in this illusion and by paying homage to it, we forsake the power we all have within us to be something greater than what we can yet perceive. Only those who have crossed this cognitive threshold can see the vast potential landscape that awaits an awakened humanity and what we may become as a species. Jesus' kingdom of Heaven still awaits us, empty and barren for humanity's unwillingness to change itself.

The illusion keeps us ensnared in sameness, in corrals that only hobble our consciousness and keep us ever enslaved to the illusion's mandates that we perceive ourselves as lesser beings, always subject to someone in 'authority', never becoming our own authority. The only salvation to be found is from within yourself, not some external supernatural force that will magically give it to you for free for the professing of a mere *belief*. Yet, it is the persistent belief in the illusion of external salvation and authoritarianism that keeps humanity bound in servitude, never advancing and always chasing the outer adornments of the next new illusionary system of mystical beliefs.

Nietzsche's distaste of the corruption of Jesus' teachings is evident in this later passage from *The Antichrist*:

*"— Our age is proud of its historical sense: how could it make believable the nonsense that at the beginning of Christianity there stands the **crude miracle-worker and savior fable** — and that everything spiritual and symbolic is only a later development? On the contrary: the history of Christianity — and that beginning in fact with the death on the cross — is the history of the step by step, ever cruder misunderstanding of an **original** symbolism. With every diffusion of Christianity over still broader, still rawer masses in whom the*

*presuppositions out of which it was born are ever
more lacking it became more necessary to
vulgarize, to **barbarize** Christianity — it has
gulped down the doctrines and rites of all the
subterranean cults of the **imperium Romanum**,
gulped down the nonsense of all kinds of sick
reason. The fate of Christianity lies in the necessity
that its faith had to itself become as sick, as low
and vulgar, as the necessities it was meant to
satisfy were sick, low, and vulgar. In the character
of the Church this **sick barbarism** itself added up
to power — the Church, this form of deadly enmity
to all integrity, to all **loftiness** of the soul, to all
cultivation of the spirit, to all candid and kind
humanity. The **Christian** values — the **noble**
values: only we, we **free-gotten** spirits, have
restored this greatest value-antithesis there is! —"*

[Emphasis in original]

With the clarifying information provided in this book
about how the messages of the true messengers to humanity have
had their voices silenced with overlaid doctrines of dependency
and institutionalized sameness, can anyone truly find fault with
Nietzsche's observations of the corruption he clearly and fairly
scorns? Nietzsche' vision saw through the illusion that I have
emphasized in this book. I am not going to synopsize his
realizations for they need to be digested in full. Humanity needs
to swallow this pill of reality once and for all and face its folly

before it can ever advance as a species. Again, from *The Antichrist*:

> *— I will go back, I will tell the **true** story of Christianity. — The word "Christianity" is already a misunderstanding — , in reality there has only been one Christian, and he died on the cross. The "Evangel" **died** on the cross. What was called "Evangel" from this moment on was already the opposite of what **he** had lived: "**bad tidings**," a dysangel. It is false to the point of nonsense to see in a "belief," perhaps the belief in salvation through Christ, the mark of distinction of a Christian: only Christian practice, a life such as he who died on the cross **lived**, is Christian ... **Such** a life is possible still today, for **certain** men even necessary: the true, the original Christianity will be possible at all times ... **Not** a believing but a doing, a **not**-doing-much above all, another kind of **being** ... States of consciousness, any kind of belief, a holding-something-for-true for example — every psychologist knows this — are fifth-rate and matters of complete indifference indeed compared to the value of the instincts: speaking more strictly, the whole concept of spiritual causality is false. To reduce being a Christian, Christianness, to a holding-something-for-true, to a mere phenom-enalism of consciousness, means to negate*

*Christianness. **In reality there have been no Christians at all**. The "Christian," that which has been called Christian for the last two thousand years, is merely a psychological self-misunderstanding. Looked at more closely, **despite** all belief it is **merely** the instincts which have prevailed in him — and what instincts! — "Belief" has been at all times, for example in Luther; only a cloak, a cover, a **curtain** behind which the instincts played their game —, a clever **blindness** about the dominance of **certain** instincts... "Belief" — I have already called it the true Christian **shrewdness**, — one always spoke of "belief," one always **acted** only out of instinct ... In the Christian world of ideas there is nothing that even touches upon reality: on the other hand, we have recognized in the instinctive hatred **toward** reality the driving force, the only driving force at the root of Christianity. What follows from this? That in **psychologicis** as well the error here is radical, that is, essence-determining, that is, a matter of **substance**. **One** concept removed here, a single reality put in its place — and the whole of Christianity crumbles into nothingness! Viewed from a height, this strangest of all facts, a religion dependent on errors but inventive and even ingenious only through destructive, **only** through life- and heart-poisoning errors, remains a* *spectacle for the gods* — *for those deities who are at the same time philosophers and whom I have encountered, for example, during those famous dialogues on Naxos. The moment **nausea** leaves them (— **and** leaves us!), they are thankful for the Christian spectacle: perhaps only for the sake of **this** curious case that pitiful star called earth deserves a divine glance, a bit of divine interest ... For let us not underrate the Christian: the Christian, **false to the point of innocence**, is far above the ape — with regard to Christians a well-known theory of descent becomes mere politeness.''*

[Emphasis in original]

Is there any more well-deserved polemic against the blindness of the human herds, those herds who follow blindly whichever authority happens to be in power at the moment, whether secular or religious? In his time, there was no New Age spiritual movement. Madame Blavatsky's writings were only then beginning to reach the public to spread an equally devastating cognitive plague similar to Christianity called Theosophy, the seed designed to uproot and supplant Christianity with the next mystical doctrine of dependency predicated on the belief in the supernatural. It was one mystical religion's supplanting of another, adorned in new raiments of ancient pagan occult practices and metaphysics, all wrapped up in a pretty new package to sell the spiritually-hungry public. Just as Christianity of the Roman

Church variety subsumed the rites and rituals of its pagan religious competitors to create the goulash called Christianity, Theosophy followed the selfsame agenda working to subsume all the religions of the world under the umbrella of its new mystical doctrine, selling Ascended Masters in the same package as the angels of old with some aliens thrown in for some additional mystical flavoring, no different than a box of mixed chocolates.

Roman Christianity showed how it was done. Theosophy and its offspring, the New Age Movement, merely continued with the same game providing mystical salvation and peddling the same 'humans as lesser beings to some mystical higher power' doctrine as did Christianity before it. If the road to this deception was graded by Christianity, it was finally paved with Theosophical New Ageism and the modern spiritual movement. Both are cut from the same handicapping cloth of humanity's dependency and trust in anything but itself.

Just as Buddha took aim at the dominant priestly religion of control of Hinduism during his life, and Jesus took aim at the Synagogue and other public pagan practices during his life, Nietzsche zeroed in on Christianity as the dominant mind-controlling mystical force of his era. These men were all the same insofar as the messages they carried for humanity, and the swords they used to tear at the structures of the tyranny were their tongues. Today we have the added dimension of the New Age spiritual movement spawned by Theosophy, and it is due every bit as much polemic and scorn as all its mystical predecessors, for it is part and parcel of the same cognitive tyranny. Don't think for a minute that Islam is exempt from this criticism, for its very name exposes what that supernatural religion is all about – *Submission!* In that respect, it is only Christianity's cousin, another mystical religion sprung from the same poisoned soil of Judaism.

The following passage from *The Antichrist* precedes the last one, but it must be included here, for Nietzsche's distaste of Christianity in the 19th century is even more relevant today in the information era where New Ageism produces drug store gurus by the score. The priests of the old Church are still alive and well, but to them must be added the modern sowers of holy lies, the New Age gurus and fake shamans. What Nietzsche wrote then is only amplified now in the computer age. Expand his criticism of Christianity below to include Islam and the entire modern spiritual movement and one begins to see the truer picture of a cognitive tyranny that is staggeringly mind boggling in its scope.

*— At this point I do not suppress a sigh. There are days when a feeling blacker than the blackest melancholy visits me — the **contempt for man**. And to leave no doubt about **what** I despise, **whom** I despise: it is the man of today, the man with whom I am fatefully contemporary. The man of today — I choke on his unclean breath... Towards the past I have, like all knowledgeable ones, a great tolerance, that is to say, a **magnanimous** self-control: I pass through the madhouse-world of whole millennia, whether it be called "Christianity," "Christian belief," "Christian Church" with a gloomy caution — I*

*take care not to make mankind answerable for its mental disorders. But my feeling changes, breaks out, as soon as I enter the modern age, **our** age. Our age is **aware**... What was formerly just sick has today become indecent — it is indecent to be a Christian today. **And here begins my disgust**. — I look around me: there is not a word left anymore of what was formerly called "truth," we cannot stand it anymore if a priest so much as utters the word "truth." Even with the most modest claim to integrity one **must** know today that a theologian, a priest, a pope, with every sentence he speaks, not only errs, but **lies** — that he is no longer free to lie out of "innocence," out of "ignorance." Also the priest knows, as well as everyone knows, that there is no "God" anymore, no "sins," no "Savior" — that "free will," "moral world-order" are **lies** — seriousness, profound self-overcoming of the spirit no longer **permits** anyone **not** to know about this ... All the concepts of the Church are recognized for what they are, the most **malicious** counterfeiting there is, for the purpose of **devaluing** nature and natural values; the priest himself is recognized for what he is, the most dangerous kind of parasite, the true poison-spider of life ... We know, our **conscience** knows it today — , **what** those sinister inventions of the priest and the Church are generally worth, to what end they have served in* *attaining that condition of mankind's self-violation, the view of which is enough to make a person sick — the concepts "other world," "Last Judgment," "immortality of the soul," the "soul" itself: they are instruments of torture, they are forms of cruelty by virtue of which the priest became master, remained master... Everybody knows this:* **and in spite of this everything remains as before.** *Where have the last feelings of decency, of self-respect gone when even our statesmen, an otherwise very unbiased kind of men and anti-Christians in deed through and through, still call themselves Christians today and go to communion? ... A young prince at the head of his regiment, magnificent as the expression of his people's egotism and self-conceit — but* **without** *any shame in professing himself a Christian!* **Whom** *then does Christianity deny?* **What** *does it call "world"? That one is a soldier, that one is a judge, that one is a patriot; that one defends himself; that one stands upon his honor; that one desires his advantage; that one is* **proud** *... every practice of every moment, every instinct, every valuation which becomes deed is today anti-Christian: What a* **monstrosity of falsity** *the modern man must be, that in spite of this he is still* **not ashamed** *to call himself a Christian!"*

[Emphasis in original]

We do not rail at the gods, we rail at a complacent and lazy humanity that refuses to pull itself up by the bootstraps and become something more than it is. The incessant reliance on the mystical and magical, the desire to escape what could be a better life and to utterly shun *life* as a human being is the present curse of humanity. To do this, to embrace these mystical notions of human unworthiness *makes* humanity unworthy to call itself human. Humans live their lives as drones, no more than cogs in an infernal machine, who either strive to climb the ladder of authoritarianism so they can direct and rule their petty ego fiefdoms, or who seek escape from being a worker drone to become a mystical spiritual drone.

The illusion keeps us ensnared in sameness, in corrals that only hobble our consciousness and keep us ever enslaved to the illusion's mandates that we perceive ourselves as lesser beings, always subject to someone in 'authority', never becoming our own authority. Since it was the early Hindu priestly elite who had the boldness to move in behind Buddha after his death and reshape his dangerous teachings into those of a supreme docility and subservience to their god concept of Brahman, mixing Hindu philosophy with Buddhist teachings, these opportunists took teachings of personal responsibility and self-reliance and turned Buddha's teachings into a mystical swill of spiritual dependency where its acolytes are ever seeking and never finding anything.

Instead of Buddha's teachings that provided answers, they turned Buddhism into a religion of relentless riddles and questions, the answers to which, to this day, their priests and gurus cannot provide because they do not possess either the knowledge or the wisdom to know what those teachings meant. The priests and gurus of both these mystical religions are mere philosophers, ignorant speculators deceitfully passing themselves off as wise sages, which is why both religions are considered philosophical in nature. Of philosophers, Nietzsche wrote in *Human, All too Human*:

"All philosophers have the common failing of starting out from man as he is now and thinking they can reach their goal through an analysis of him. They involuntarily think of 'man' as an **aeterna veritas** *[something everlastingly true], as something that remains constant in the midst of all flux, as a sure measure of things. Everything the philosopher has declared about man is, however, at bottom no more than a testimony as to the man of a very* **limited** *period of time. Lack of historical sense is the family failing of all philosophers; many, without being aware of it, even take the most recent manifestation of man, such as has arisen under the impress of certain religions, even certain political events, as the fixed form from which one has to start out. They will not learn that man has become, that the faculty of cognition has become; while some of them would have it* **<u>that the whole world is spun out of this faculty of cognition</u>**. *Now, everything* **essential** *in the development of*

*mankind took place in primeval times, long before the four thousand years we more or less know about; during these years mankind may well not have altered very much. But the philosopher here sees 'instincts' in man as he now is and assumes that these belong to the unalterable facts of mankind and to that extent could provide a key to the understanding of the world in general: the whole of teleology is constructed by speaking of the man of the last four millennia as of an **eternal** man towards whom all things in the world have had a natural relationship from the time he began. But everything has become: there are no **eternal** **facts**, just as there are no absolute truths. Consequently what is needed from now on is **historical philosophizing**, and with it the virtue of modesty."*

[Bold emphasis in original]
[Underlined bold mine]

In this passage Nietzsche hits the nail squarely on the head, and I have made similar observations in my other works, particularly when criticizing Psychology, which is the bastard offspring of Philosophy. The baseline of measurement of all present philosophy, including the religious philosophies of the East, is that of a single system of cognition which is used as a baseline for measurement and determination; to wit, the first cognition system of awareness. Psychology arrogantly and erroneously calls this baseline of measure 'human nature', but it is *not* human nature. It is a system of limited cognitive awareness which is controlled and governed by the ego, the false self.

Any experiment has to have a baseline for measuring change, but if the baseline is a falsely 'assumed' given, then any results, any philosophical or psychological determinations reached from that erroneous baseline must, accordingly, be in error as well. This is the great failing of philosophers as well as the field of Psychology. What they presume to be human nature is in fact a psyche infected with a parasitic virus, which is why the symptomatology reaches across the entire human cognitive spectrum.

This mind virus, as I have explained extensively in my other works, is a hive mind virus. Carl Jung was sniffing around discovering this mind virus with his Theory on the Collective Unconscious. The Collective Unconscious *is*, in fact, the hapiym virus, and because it was a virus that clustered in 'hives', it accounts for the *sameness* present in every ego consciousness worldwide. It is the symptoms of this viral infection that both philosophers and psychologists mistakenly call human nature. One cannot cure this species-wide mind virus if one refuses to see the truth of this horrible scenario, and most definitely not if they use the symptomatology of the virus as their measuring stick as the human norm.

Whether those other than don Juan knew of the virus or not, the path to cognitive freedom is the same where its requirements to destroy the false ego is concerned. Whether the reader personally wants to accept the existence of the virus habits or not, there still exists the false ego self, and it will have to be confronted and overcome if you ever expect to evolve your consciousness. Knowing that you will not 'lose yourself', since the primary ego is nothing but your true self-identity buried under the false ego, should remove this particular fear from your mind. As you can plainly tell, in the case of Friedrich Nietzsche, he did not lose who he was by ridding himself of his false ego, but instead found who he really was just as I have, and a few others have.

There are those who have speculated that Nietzsche's theories are what caused him to fall into madness in later life, but that is more likely attributable to syphilis than any condition of the mind brought about through his own development and teachings. What I have shared in this book should remove any doubt about the consistency of these teachings over the ages, regardless of how each teacher taught the principles. What these men taught is the same thing I teach in my own manner and in my own words through my other works. There is no difference in the teachings other than the manner in which each of us deliver them in our own personal style.

What Buddha, Jesus, don Juan and Nietzsche tried to teach humanity is how to overcome the symptoms of this virus and finally discover what it is to be truly human, with a consciousness free from the symptoms of this parasitic virus. The concepts and revelations I am sharing in this book provide the foundation for understanding how to cure oneself from that virus and find true cognitive freedom. All these forerunners to advanced human consciousness each provided guidelines for understanding this process of taking responsibility for oneself to overcome this ego virus and its control over our minds. These four individuals are, to my knowledge, the only four humans to ever attain cognitive freedom and have it publicly known on a broad scale, prior to myself.

Over my own years of personal growth and research, I never delved into Nietzsche's writings as one of my areas of study, but only started digging into his works in the past couple of years or so; starting with *Thus Spoke Zarathustra*, some of the quotes from which I used as instructional guides as chapter headers in my book, *Navigating Into the Second Cognition*. These passages from Nietzsche that I am sharing in this book are those that I have pulled out during research for this book, many of which I digested for the first time while writing this book. The truth of these teachings stands out glaringly to those who know how to comprehend and translate them with the correct key to understanding their value and what they say.

Before I ever read *Human, All Too Human*, I wrote my book *Willful Evolution*. You can only imagine my surprise to run across the following passage from Nietzsche's aforementioned work:

> ***Possibility of progress***. - *When a scholar of the old culture swears to have nothing more to do with people who believe in progress he is right. For the old culture has its goods and greatness behind it and history compels one to admit that it can never be fresh again; one needs to be intolerably stupid or fanatical to deny this. But men are*

[Bold emphasis in original]

[Underline emphasis mine]

What Nietzsche wrote over a century ago is the same principle about choosing to willfully evolve one's consciousness that I presented in *Willful Evolution*. Do you seriously think this is mere happenstance, especially since I had not read this passage until writing this book? What he presented in *Human, All Too Human* is no different than what I am trying to teach humanity today, and what those other forerunners of advanced consciousness tried to teach humanity 2,500 and 2,000 years ago. Their teachings left a long-lasting impression on the psyche of our species, as have the teachings of Nietzsche and don Juan in their own milieus. I am just the latest man to carry that same message to humanity. One can only imagine where humanity might be today if the messages of Buddha and Jesus had not been corrupted by institutional religion-makers who stole their messages and turned them instead into systems of cognitive slavery and mystical subservience. With this book, I am reclaiming that heritage and presenting their messages to the world for what they were meant to teach, not the corruption of dependency that they have been turned into by the priests of all ages. The cognitive lie stops here.

Error regarding life necessary to life. *-*
Every belief in the value and dignity of life rests on false thinking; it is possible only through the fact that empathy with the universal life and suffering of mankind is very feebly developed in the individual. Even those rarer men who think beyond themselves at all have an eye, not for this universal life, but for fenced-off portions of it. If one knows how to keep the exceptions principally in view, I mean the greatly gifted and pure of soul, takes their production for the goal of <u>world-evolution</u> and

rejoices in the effects they in turn produce, one may believe in the value of life, because then one is **overlooking** *all other men: thinking falsely, that is to say. And likewise if, though one does keep in view all mankind,* <u>one accords validity only to one species of drives, the less egoistical, and justifies them in face of all the others, then again one can hope for something of mankind as a whole and to this extent believe in the value of life</u>*: thus, in this case too, through falsity of thinking. Whichever of these attitudes one adopts, however, one is by adopting it an* **exception** *among men. The great majority endure life without complaining overmuch; they* **believe** *in the value of existence, but they do so precisely because each of them exists for himself alone, refusing to step out of himself as those exceptions do: everything outside themselves they notice not at all or at most as a dim shadow. Thus for the ordinary, everyday man the value of life rests solely on the fact that he regards himself more highly than he does the world. The great lack of imagination from which he suffers means he is unable to feel his way into other beings and thus he participates as little as possible in their fortunes and sufferings.* **He***, on the other hand, who really could participate in them would have to despair of the value of life; if he succeeded in encompassing and feeling within himself the total* *consciousness of mankind he would collapse with a curse on existence - for mankind has as a whole no goal, and the individual man when he regards its total course cannot derive from it any support or comfort, but must be reduced to despair. If in all he does he has before him the ultimate goallessness of man, his actions acquire in his own eyes the character of useless squandering. But to feel thus* **squandered**, *not merely as an individual but as humanity as a whole, in the way we behold the individual fruits of nature squandered, is a feeling beyond all other feelings. - But who is capable of such a feeling? Certainly only a poet: and poets always know how to console themselves.*

[Emphasis in original]

[Underlined emphasis mine]

What the foregoing passage describes is the selfishness and self-interested focus of a man and a culture driven solely by the ego false self through the continual process of false thinking. It is through such false thinking and ego self-glorification that humanity's consciousness remains in a state of arrested development. The latter half of the passage describes the realization process that the destruction of the false ego can lead to as one's process unfolds and they come face to face with the lie they thought was reality. Reaching this state, in some, could lead to a sense of nihilism, and many have accused Nietzsche of being a Nihilist. By being so blunt in presenting this truth of the process,

Nietzsche explained what we must each transition through on the road to the second cognition. This sense of nihilism is one that everyone passes through on this road, and is only a phase that one can transcend if they do not fall into ego self-indulgence and self-pity and become permanent, whining nihilists. Recognizing the truth is not the same as transcending it into wisdom.

Much of what Nietzsche relates here is the bouts of cognitive dissonance one goes through during this process of deconstructing the false ego. Since the Theory of Cognitive Dissonance was not put forth until 1957 by Leon Festinger, Nietzsche didn't have this psychological terminology to fall back on to support the explanations of the process he elucidates in the foregoing passage, as well as others throughout his extensive body of work. What the field of Psychology has yet to realize is that to create cognitive resonance, ridding oneself of the false ego, its beliefs and perceptual lies about its illusionary reality, is the basis for cognitive dissonance in the first place. It is when one faces the truth over their believed perceptual lies that cognitive dissonance occurs and creates the psychological crisis that facing the truth brings to and overshadows false beliefs. Cognitive resonance occurs when the false ego's lies and beliefs are *shed* and the truth begins to rule one's psyche. When the process of deconstructing the false ego is complete, one attains a state of 'balance' and cognitive equanimity that Buddha taught about; what all too many believers in institutionalized Buddhism think is a state of 'divine bliss'. When the individual reaches this state of cognitive equilibrium, they are no longer emotionally reactive in the same sense that the false ego reacts to anything that challenges is perceptual reality. Of this state of cognitive peace, Jesus said in Philippians 4:6-8

> *"6 Be anxious for nothing, but in everything, by prayer and petition, with thanksgiving, present your requests to God.*
>
> *7 And the peace of God, which surpasses all understanding, will guard your hearts and your minds in Christ Jesus.*
>
> *8 Finally, brothers, whatever is true, whatever is honorable, whatever is right, whatever is pure, whatever is lovely, whatever is admirable—if anything is excellent or praiseworthy—think on these things. ..."*

With the explanations I have provided thus far in this book, can these teachings become any more clear and understandable? Can the reader now understand Nietzsche's proclamation in *Ecce Homo* for his teachings in *Thus Spoke Zarathustra*? Are these the words of an arrogant man, or a new kind of human that we can each *become* if we but embark on this journey and stay the course to completion.

> *"— Among my writings my Zarathustra stands by itself. With this book I have given mankind the greatest gift it has ever been given. This book, with a voice that carries over millennia, is not only the highest book that there is, the true*

mountain-air book — the whole fact of man lies at a tremendous distance beneath it — it is also the deepest book, born out of the innermost abundance of truth, an inexhaustible well into which no bucket descends without coming up filled with gold and goodness. Here it is not a "prophet" who speaks, not one of those horrible hybrids of sickness and will to power people call founders of religions. Above all, one must correctly hear the tone that issues from this mouth, this halcyon tone, so as not to do pitiful injustice to the sense of its wisdom. "It is the stillest words that bring on the storm. Thoughts that come on doves' feet rule the world — ""…….

"Here no fanatic speaks, here nothing is "preached," here no belief is demanded: from an endless abundance of light and depth of happiness falls drop after drop, word after word — the tempo of these speeches is a tender adagio. Such things reach only the most select; it is a privilege without equal to be a listener here; no one is simply free to have ears for Zarathustra…So is Zarathustra not a seducer?…But what does he himself say when for the first time he again returns to his solitude? Exactly the opposite of what any "sage," "saint," "world savior" and other décadent would say in

Oh, ye pompous and ego-inflated philosophers, can your ears now hear his true message? Can ye breathe that clear mountain air of his understanding after more than a century of philosophical speculation and intellectual mind-twisting that, to this day, has yielded ye no fruit of wisdom? Do ye yet perceive the measure of the man of controversy, of madness? Methinks not so.

The works of Friedrich Nietzsche should be viewed as a catalogue of his own personal journey to enlightenment – his triumphs and turmoil as he plumbed the depths of his own psyche to defeat his own ego demons, until that moment of his crossing over into the second cognition occurred when Zarathustra "overcame him". His collected works are a catalogue of his personal journey, just as every individual will have to embark on their own personal journey. At every turn, the false ego will try to destroy each and every one of you through fear and doubt and internal conflict, and one can lose this battle anywhere along the way that they give up on themselves and the process. In regard to this process, one should pay close heed to Nietzsche's words, again from *Human, All Too Human*:

"The whole of human life is sunk deeply in untruth; the individual cannot draw it up out of this well without thereby growing profoundly disillusioned about his own past, without finding his present motives, such as that of honour, absurd, and pouring mockery and contempt on the passions which reach out to the future and promise happiness in it. Is it true, is all that remains a mode of thought whose outcome on a personal level is despair and on a theoretical level a philosophy of destruction? – I believe that the nature of the after-effect of knowledge is determined by a man's temperament: in addition to the after-effect described I could just as easily imagine a different one, quite possible in individual instances, <u>by virtue of which a life could arise much simpler and emotionally cleaner than our present life is:</u> so that, though the old motives of violent desire produced by inherited habit would still possess their strength, they would gradually grow weaker under the influence of purifying knowledge. In the end one would live among men and with oneself as in nature, without praising, blaming, contending, gazing contentedly, as though at a spectacle, upon many things for which one formerly felt only fear. One would be free of emphasis, and no longer

prodded by the idea that one is only nature or more
than nature".

[Underlined emphasis mine]

What is expressed in this passage is the whole first cognition consciousness. It is a world where people *choose* to wallow in the iniquity of untruth for the sake of preserving a world of illusion. In this world, humanity will fight, defend and kill one another to preserve a planet-wide falsehood, with each human herd's falsehood proclaimed to be the 'one true way', whether that way is religious, political, national or cultural. When viewed from a higher perspective, from a state of wisdom and not the bravado of false knowing, one can only view our species with disdain, with a disgust in the knowing that it can be changed if people will only choose to make that change by starting with changing themselves first.

As with all inversions in that perceptual world of illusions ruled by the hive-minded ego, we do not have to steer the herds first, but must take the helm of ourselves before any larger changes on a planetary scale will every take place. You have no control over the herds, unless of course you are one of the self-designated elite controllers of first cognition consciousness – the magicians and manipulators of the mass human cognitive illusion. How arrogant the ego is to envision itself a hero, here to save humanity by creating doctrines for followers to something as petty as a *cause*. What a pinnacle of self-aggrandizement the ego presents to the presumed hero, here to save the world, when its very consciousness cannot save itself! What greater self-illusion can one entertain?

Mankind has not learned that advancement is not dictated from the top down in hierarchal systems of authoritarianism where the few control the many. Advancement as a species must come from the bottom up, from the everyman who chooses to walk the road of becoming his own overman, the successors over the world of the illusion; the ones who can not only face reality, but who can accept reality and become wise human beings. When humans decide to actually learn from the errors of the past and stop repeating them, then we may change as a species. Continually embracing and feeding the ego's world of illusion has led our species to the brink of another world war as competing ego herds vie for supremacy just one more time.

Blessed are the peacemakers – those who can find their own internal peace and serve as living examples to others that fruitlessly seek peace from outside agencies, for these peacemakers are the ones who present real peace – the peace of knowing not only who they are, but who also know the illusion for what it is and can walk through the storm of the illusion and live their lives despite the turmoil that surround them. We are the eye of the hurricane, that place of rest amidst all the doubt and fear that surrounds us. You have a choice as to which of these worlds you want to live in and experience, you always have. Are your ears listening now, or will you continue to bluster and justify the hateful illusion as just another defender of the first cognition *faith*?

There is only one thing that deserves any kind of faith, and that is the faith in oneself, not as just another blustering ego, but as one who truly knows who they are; one who requires no illusions to support their own false ego self-image - a person of strength begotten from truly knowing oneself and not a petty false *persona* driven by fear and doubt-ridden arrogance. The ego mind is but a knock-off, a proxy consciousness which has substituted itself for the real thing. And like any knock-off, it cannot pass the test of scrutiny and time – it is not genuine and will always lack that quality of genuineness. Do you want to continue to be the counterfeit of yourself, or transcend the faux consciousness of the cognitive con artist? That is the choice every one of us faces, if we will only choose our real selves over the fraud. There is only one thing that needs salvation, and that is saving the real you from the white-knuckled clutches of the false ego. No god or divine entity can provide this salvation, only you can, and it will never be done if you don't make the choice to start on this journey and see it through.

These are words of wisdom and truth. They only push one belief, and that is the belief in yourself. That is the *only* belief required. It's all that was ever required. If you want to fight for a cause, put your efforts into fighting your ego for your true self. You will never find a more capable, lying, deceitful or dangerous enemy than this. If you can't conquer your own inner adversary, then you are not qualified to do anything more than perpetuate its illusionary reality and remain a slave to it – just another defender the faith of the illusion.

5. A BRIEF SUMMARY OF DON JUAN

Based on modern copyright restrictions and the legal wrangling over permissions (not to mention the cost), I am unable to quote don Juan's teachings as extensively as I can from public domain material within this book, so I am going to offer a brief summary and provide a link to an educational website for those interested in reading his teachings separated and excerpted from the storytelling of Carlos Castenada. I have recently released a book called *Clarifying the Don Juan Teachings for the Second Cognition* which is available for a free .pdf download at our we website at http://www.demystifyingthemystical.com/#/ which is a comprehensive addition to this chapter where I treat the don Juan teachings extensively as I have the other teachers in this book.

As noted within these pages, every teacher for cognitive advancement developed their own styles and methods to relate these teachings. Although the core teachings remain the same, the different methods developed, or the means through which these teachings were offered varied from individual to individual. Some developed 'exercises' that they felt would help break the ego's stranglehold on their student's consciousness, and others chose the word through which to relate their ideas.

Although it was not stated in Carlos Castenada's books, it is obvious that he was on a personal mystical quest. He was seeking the magical experience, like virtually every other person on the modern spiritual path rife with gurus and shamans at every turn. It was Castenada's books, using don Juan's teaching as his platform, that introduced the presumed 'shamanic' aspect of these teachings to the public. From what is presented in this book, one should now be fully aware that none of these teachers, including don Juan, promoted drug use as a shortcut to enlightenment. Yet the magical stories fabricated by Castenada had a far-reaching and negative effect on these teachings, no different than the poison sown by the priesthoods of old that misdirected people away from the teachings of Buddha and Jesus.

I have gone to great lengths in my other books in exposing the Fabian Society, which was founded in England before Nietzsche died. I will not rehash all that information here, but only use this to point out that the use of LSD and other psychedelic mind-altering drugs to achieve a mystical state of enlightenment was forwarded by the Fabian, Aldous Huxley, also pushed by the rock and roll era guru Timothy Leary, and was finally pushed into the spiritual arena with Castenada's writings. The British Fabian Society also has an incestuous relationship with the Theosophical Society which, after the death of its founder, Madame Helena Blavatsky, was taken over in America by the Fabian, Alice Bailey.

Be that as it may, there is a hidden agenda behind present New Ageism and it is not all that it presents itself to be to the public at large and to all those spiritual seekers who embrace its tenets. Although there were some New Age ideas floating around in the 50's and 60's, they were inconsequential compared to Castenada's tales of his own purported drug-induced trips to enlightenment land through the teachings of don Juan that really gave New Ageism its impetus in the 60's and 70's and allowed it to develop into a full blown alternative religion in the 1980's.

The 60's sex, drug and rock & roll era provided fertile ground for the works of Castenada to take off and grow. Unfortunately, it was his tales of drug-induced fantasies and magical prowess seeking enlightenment that captivated the mind of the public, mine included. Don Juan and his teachings played a secondary role to Castenada's own lack of understanding those teachings and, once again, the truth of these teachings was exchanged for lies fabricated by one man's ego. Castenada's own stupendous ego prevented him from *ever* understanding these teachings other than on the barest superficial scale.

Castenada's impact on public perception was so widespread that he was actually featured on the cover of Time magazine in March of 1973, with the enticing proclamation on the cover, "Carlos Castenada: Magic and Reality". Magic became the focus of his work, and not the pragmatic teachings of don Juan. This misdirection by Castenada made his fame and fortune and created the desire in every mystical seeker after enlightenment using drugs as the shortcutting vehicle to his cause, to line up like rats behind the Pied Piper. Naturally, these magical practices were grafted into the overall Theosophical, occult, New Age tapestry without so much as a hiccup. The truth that don Juan tried to provide was supplanted with mystical nonsense, no different than how the truth of all the other teachers was hijacked by mystical religions before him, excepting Nietzsche, who was conveniently blackballed to silence his voice during his lifetime.

Although it was never revealed in any of his books, the astute observer can see that Castenada did not get all of his teachings from don Juan, but was more realistically 'shaman shopping' across Mexico and searching for what pacified his own ego's lust for magical power and fame. I have yet to see any other researcher into Castenada's work make this connection. Given the probable scenario that he was in fact shaman shopping, taking what he wanted from this shaman or that, the teachings that left the most lasting effect on his psyche were those of don Juan, because he knew there was power in them, but he could never figure it out. Because they were a never-solved mystery for him, too deep for his own ego to understand, he used don Juan and his teachings to concoct his own mystical stories with Castenada as the star.

There are enough of don Juan's true teachings that managed to get through Castenada's editing, even though he did not restrict himself from putting words of other shamans in don Juan's mouth, that the truths he taught still stand in silent testimony to his teachings. Until one can see through this manipulation, they can't separate the real core teachings from Castenada's intentional and fraudulent misdirection. What has survived the editing pen of Castenada's over-creative imagination is the truth that neither he nor those who are still seeking to comprehend those core teachings can understand. Don Juan's core teachings are as much a mystery to first cognition humans as are the teachings of Buddha, Jesus and the writings of Nietzsche. It was exactly because they ever remained a mind-bending mystery to Castenada that he used those teachings as a foundation to glorify himself as the next guru, then next sorcerer, or *Nagual*, to replace don Juan. Such an arrogant travesty by an over-inflated ego can scarcely be imagined.

To separate the teachings from the storytelling, one must see what was attributed to don Juan without the magical tales of adventure that Castenada concocted around himself. The person who created the website below has taken the time to separate the lion's share of these teachings from the storytelling in Castenada's books so others can try and learn from them. But aside from separating the teachings attributed to don Juan at their face value as presented in Castenada's books, one must further separate these teachings from others that Castenada drew from other shamans, and those are the additions about drug use. When this is all stripped away, then one arrives at what don Juan taught.

http://www.prismagems.com/castaneda/

Don Juan used exercises he developed as a form of concentration to try and break Carlos from his mental habits of thinking too much. The exercises themselves were nothing more than focus tools to try and break first cognition indoctrinated thinking habits. Beyond this purpose, those exercises have no merit is some kind of mystical pathway to enlightenment, yet Castenada so misunderstood the teachings and the purposes of the exercises that he eventually created the process he called Tensegrity and sold to the masses as a process that would lead to enlightenment if practiced. This is no different than Hindus and Buddhists practicing Yoga thinking that those exercises are part of attaining enlightenment. Physical exercises of this nature in and of themselves provide none of the requirements for cognitive advancement. They are merely accoutrements, and outer dressing at best that, unfortunately, deceived too many humans for all too long.

If one reads the don Juan material and chooses to try these exercises, which are really unnecessary in this process, just know what their purpose was as a focus tool designed to distract the ego mind long enough to just plain shut up in your head. The practice of meditation utilized by Buddha was the same kind of focus tool which worked for him to help him silence his own mind and shut down the voice of his own ego. It was never used by Buddha to "connect to the Divine."

The understand the don Juan teachings we must work to separate the tone of mysticism that is pervasive in all of Castenada's books. For those who have studied the material over the years, the magical and fanciful storytelling of Castenada is a clear and present danger to gleaning the wisdom from the teachings. These stories create a heavy fog that prevents the students of don Juan's teachings from seeing them clearly for what they present. Because every teacher of higher cognitive awareness is a slave to teaching in allegory because the first cognition system of understanding simply has no means to comprehend what is beyond its ken, the added elements of mysticism make these allegories even harder to comprehend. The damage that Castenada did to these teachings is equally as abhorrent as what the priesthoods of old did who corrupted and institutionalized false interpretations of Jesus and Buddha.

One thing we do have to thank Castenada for is for getting these teachings out to the public at all, even at the cost of his own fraudulent storytelling. There have been many critics over the years who made it a career to expose Castenada for the fraud artist that he was. The most vocal of these critics was Richard de Mille, and his writings on the subject of Carlos Castenada are very revealing in themselves. De Mille was totally convinced that the character don Juan was non-existent, simply being a figment of Castenada's wild imagination. Regardless of de Mille's assertions, however, what proves that a person existed, whether actually named don Juan or not, was not a fabrication of Castenada's imagination, is that these teachings are too profound for those who understand them to have been fabricated by a mere hoax artist and plagiarist controlled by his own ego.

Had the don Juan teachings been a fabrication of Castenada's imagination, then he most assuredly didn't live up to what the teachings presented about *impeccability*, for Castenada had no impeccability. When reading Nietzsche, we find that he often uses the word integrity, which in his case should be considered the same as don Juan's impeccability, although this author sees a distinction between the two words. Impeccability means to be true to one's inner self, whereas in the first cognition world, one may possess integrity and still uphold false beliefs that form this integrity. This is where impeccability and integrity differ, and it does not amount to simple hair-splitting over the definitions of two words. I will give a free pass to Nietzsche based on what he had attained in higher awareness for using the word integrity instead of impeccability because he knew what he meant by using the word, whereas most first cognition thinkers can't see the difference. So, when you read Nietzsche and you find the word integrity in his writings, you can safely insert the word impeccability and do no harm to his teachings.

Just as I have gone to great lengths to describe the difference between first second cognition consciousness, don Juan did the same in his own fashion. As noted earlier, he used the word *tonal* to describe the first cognition world of perception, and the word *nagual* to describe the second system of higher consciousness He stated plainly in his teachings that they were two distinct and separate systems of cognition. It doesn't get any clearer than that. Unfortunately, because of the mystical stories presented by Castenada, and his insistence that psychedelic drug use led to this altered state of awareness, the second system of cognitive awareness that don Juan taught has been misconstrued to be a mystical altered state of awareness. It's not.

If you are doing mind-altering drugs, they do create an altered (drug-induced) state of awareness compared to sober, waking consciousness, but this altered state does not lead to an advanced state of cognitive awareness. It merely makes our synaptic network go nuts, creating hallucinations and presumed mystical experiences. It is definitely an 'altered state', but it flies in the face of what don Juan taught about this process, and that is the necessity of *sobriety* and *pragmatism* in this work. To take on the task of dismantling one's system of beliefs to finally see through the illusion is a very sobering task to say the least. It has to be done pragmatically to be successful as well. So, I ask any student of Castenada's stories ho may be reading this volume, how does getting high and seeing hallucinations cross-foot with what don Juan taught about sobriety and pragmatism? The fact is, it doesn't.

Where the teachings of don Juan appear to venture into the mystical for most people is when he endeavors to explain the 'inorganic beings' and the 'predators'. Using the first cognition framework of defining reality in the rigid terms it does, the mind races to the exit when such ideas are presented to them. It all sounds too much like science fiction or fantasy to accept at first gloss. Yet we find clues of this same aspect of reality in Buddha's teachings in his battle with the armies of Mara. Philosophers and materialists would prefer that such stories as these be relegated to the dustbin of mythology, and unfortunately, that is where don Juan's instruction on the inorganics gets trashed as well. It goes beyond the scope of this presentation to delve into this topic in any depth, but it is covered in some of my other works – *We Are Not Alone – Part 3: The Luciferian Agenda of the Mother Goddess, Revamping Psychology: A Critique of Transpersonal Psychology* and *The Energetic War Against Humanity: The 6,000 Year War Against Human Cognitive Advancement,* for those interested in pursuing further research into this subject.

The work don Juan sought to guide Castenada through is no different than what these other teaches taught where overcoming the ego, what don Juan called one's 'person', is concerned. Where don Juan differs from Nietzsche, in particular, is in the fact of what he presented in regard to what he called 'infinity'. In the greater context for the reader's understanding, infinity is the larger reality of the universe in which we live, about which humans know next to nothing, regardless of the claims of scientism to have a handle on that reality. Had Nietzsche lived longer, he may have reached these frontiers, but there is little visible evidence in this writings that he did, although he did speculate that there were other unexplored options available once one transitioned into this higher state of cognitive awareness. All science is presently based on materialist ideas and relies completely on the five-senses that humanity uses in the first cognition as its singular system of perceptual measurement. With the exception, perhaps, of quantum physics, all our so-called sciences are founded upon and operate within this same limited system of perceptual measurement, which is why advanced consciousness can't be understood, because it opens the door to an entirely different world of perceptual and cognitive awareness which materialist scientism simply denies exists as a possibility.

The teachings don Juan left about infinity and the *nagual* are the doors that open to understanding the universe at large. There is no mysticism, no God, no Divine Oneness and no overarching consciousness suggested in any of don Juan's teachings. All such ideas are for those seeking dependency on a higher source for whatever variety of salvation or rescue that they are seeking. As with the other teachers, don Juan taught the self-sufficiency of the individual as his own higher power. His more esoteric-sounding teachings were designed to give people who understood is work, the pragmatic preparations for what they would eventually encounter as a 'spirit warrior', using his terminology, when those doors to infinity opened up. I can attest to the fact that these teachings are not erroneous, having experienced 'infinity' myself. Don Juan was totally correct when he instructed Castenada that such an undertaking takes extreme sobriety and pragmatism. There is nothing fanciful about the universe at large, and humanity at this stage of its development is totally unprepared to deal with it.

I am not going to go through all the things that don Juan taught on a point by point basis, for it is beyond the scope of this book to do so. But for those of his students who are still seeking to know the meanings in what he taught, this chapter, combined with reading *Clarifying the don Juan Teachings for the Second Cognition,* should remove any doubt that what he taught in his own style is no different than the principles about cognitive advancement taught by other teachers highlighted in this presentation.

6. YOUR OWN PATH

Just as Nietzsche gifted the world with *Thus Spoke Zarathustra* to guide humanity forward in understanding itself, this book stands in the same caliber as that work. I am no more ashamed to acknowledge the power in this book to change the world of those who have been seeking their own form of enlightenment than Nietzsche claimed for *Zarathustra.* There is no false hubris or arrogance in my claiming this. It is simply a statement of what is. Those who have the ears to hear will hear and do whatever is necessary to discover who they really are within, and step into the power that comes with that knowing. For those who choose to not hear, their fates are equally in their own hands to continue their lives of illusionary folly, with their egos lying to them making them believe they know much, when in fact they know nothing except life lived in an illusion.

The book, *The Wizard of Oz,* by Frank L, Baum comes to mind when I perceive the ego world if illusion from the same high peak that Nietzsche saw the mass of humanity far below. Most people are familiar with the Hollywood production of the book, and never read Baum's book, but within the book, before one could enter the Emerald City they had to don green spectacles, which is what gave the Emerald City its green appearance. Without these spectacles, you can be assured that the walls of the magical city were as grey and dull as the world of illusion in which humanity presently lives.

Wearing the spectacles of the illusion, allegorically speaking, humanity walks through the world, its attention captured by gewgaws and electronic gadgets, chasing illusions of divine mysteries and praying to deaf, non-existent Gods, seeking to destroy anyone who disagrees with their cultural herd mandates, or vying for supremacy within their own subcultural herds and their causes. The individual ego is only a speck in the group ego mind and one can't be separated from the other, for they are all the same craven beast. All it takes to direct a human herd is a demagogue with a cause or a new religion. Find any group that is the victim and feels put-upon and you will find a herd in waiting, only waiting for the clarion call to organize into a larger beast than the victimized ego.

If you are genuinely seeking to grow into all that you can be as a fully functional human being totally responsible for yourself, operating with total impeccability, and with an unstoppable desire to discover and claim who you really are, then you are going to have to develop what don Juan called unbending intent. You are going to have to take off the emerald spectacles of the ego and see past the illusionary world you have been indoctrinated to embrace as reality. Letting go of this false reality means that you have to desire reality more than the illusion. You must choose one or the other, for these worlds are mutually exclusive. They may co-exist for a time as you unravel your own personal illusions and let go of your most cherished *beliefs*, but in the end, the illusion must die.

When one realizes that a *belief* is simply a wish, a hope that something is true, then the letting go can be easier. To continue to embrace beliefs for the simple reason that they make you feel good, or more accurately, make your ego feel good, should not be sufficient reason to continue to believe them. Yet it is this craving to feel good that drives every religion on the planet. The ego wants to live in a world where it perceives certainty, when in fact, this certainty itself is simply part of the illusion. The only certainty anyone can count on is death, yet this is the one certainty that most of humanity is seeking to escape. The tales of the afterlife paint an illusion of continuity of personality after death. It is only the ego's craving for immortality that drives this quest for mystical desires and nothing more. It all comes down to the fear of death and a supreme unwillingness to face this one certainty that every human can count on. When we can accept and face death, then the alternative to it is living life. As Nietzsche taught, we must embrace life and make of it all that we can while we live it, not squander it away chasing rainbow illusions and trading it away for promises of an afterlife or alien rescue, or escaping life by ascending to another dimension in hope of finding immortality.

Don Juan taught that we must all have death as a companion. Although I have explained this in a different vein in my other books, death is what brings us sobriety. With death as a certainty, then life is the remedy, so long as we have it. So, we must face death, make friends with it and accept it and thereby free ourselves to live life, or we lie to ourselves and seek to avoid death, which can't honestly be done, just so the ego can feel good about itself. One is living with truth, the other is living the illusion of denial.

The other aspect of the inevitably of death is found with the death of the ego. So long as we are controlled by the ego and its habits, and we are seeking to grow ourselves, the death of the ego will be our constant companion until we free ourselves from its clutches. The death of don Juan's 'person' awaits everyone on this path, and this is a death we should all rush to embrace, for it is only with the death of the hapiym ego that one finds cognitive freedom and becomes a new and different kind of human being.

As Nietzsche wrote in *Zarathustra*:

"But the worst enemy you can meet will always be yourself; you lie in wait for yourself in caverns and forests. Lonely one, you are going the way to yourself! And your way goes past yourself, and past your seven devils! You will be a heretic to yourself and witch and soothsayer and fool and doubter and unholy one and villain. You must be ready to burn yourself in your own flame: how could you become new, if you had not first become ashes?"

Don Juan taught about stalking power, and even stated that one must stalk themselves to find this power. Is this concept any different than what is stated in this passage about having to "lie in wait for yourself"? The power you seek is the power of yourself, your true self, not the false ego self which is your constant prey on this journey.

For those who have started this path and have embraced mystical notions about the Divine, the first thing you are going to have to do if you truly want to grow is face those beliefs for the fantasy they are. I implore to look at your own path, how long you have been on that path chasing these mystical illusions, and admit to yourself that they have taken you not much closer to your goal than when you started. Many of you just exchanged one set of mystical beliefs for another, no different than trying on different outfits in a clothing store. Until you are willing to face this truth, you will only continue to chase illusions, believing in some type of divine intervention to save you from yourself. The only person who can save the real you is *you*, and the only salvation necessary is from your own ego.

Although the purpose of this book has been to reclaim these teachings and redirect our perceptions down the correct path for interpreting them, what must be the most glaringly obvious is the unchanging nature of the hapiym ego virus throughout time. It has been the same within humanity since our species was infected with it until today. I have stated in my other works that the behaviors of the ego are tiresomely predictable, and from a second cognition perspective, this becomes tragically true and saddening to behold. The enemy within that you seek to overcome today is the same enemy that all these teachers overcame in their own manner. The cultural clothing may change from generation to generation, but the ego virus is ever the same.

Where the modern field of Psychology goes wrong is that it seeks to create harmony in the minds of disturbed and uncomfortable egos, seeking to heal and pacify the ego so it can fit comfortably back into its world of illusion. Psychologists, as I have stated in my other works, are nothing more than ego repairmen. As such, they are doing the world a great disservice by working to keep the illusionary world of the ego firmly in place. Only one who has transcended their own cognitive awareness beyond the world of the first cognition can see this clearly. This is why Nietzsche could write in *Ecco Homo*:

> *"That a psychologist without equal speaks from my writings – this is perhaps the first insight gained by a good reader."*

> *"Who among the philosophers before me was in any way a psychologist? Before me there simply was no psychology."*

Although Freud, Jung and Adler were all heavily influenced by Nietzsche, their own practices of psychology could not reach the pinnacle of Nietzsche's understanding of the ego. They were all men controlled by their own egos creating false assumptions and reaching erroneous conclusions from what their own egos made them believe what the ego is. These are the men who shaped modern Psychology, and as such, we find another case of Jesus' parable of the blind leading the blind and falling into a ditch because of that shared blindness. Those who came after Nietzsche in the field of psychology were mere 'wannabe's', fame-chasing, peer accepted authorities of half-baked theories and ideas that have become the mainstay for classifying 'human nature' with their own egos providing the measuring stick of that presumed human norm. Only one who has challenged and defeated their own ego is qualified to teach what it is, what its behavioral habits are, and how to transcend them. None of these other authoritative pillars of Psychology are qualified to even stand in Nietzsche's shadow where his deep understanding of the ego is concerned. Until the field of Psychology is willing to stop feeding the ego and change its focus to helping people understand it and defeat it, then the field is totally inept to do anything more than identify and nurture the symptoms of the virus, not cure it.

On your own path to cognitive advancement you have to become your own psychologist. A study of the different branches of psychology, not its presumed cures, but the identified symptomatology, could be very helpful in one identifying these behaviors in themselves so they can overcome them and defeat the hapiym virus and its habits. Denying that you do the things you are compelled to do by your own ego will not advance you. Impeccability demands that you be brutally honest with yourself in these assessments. Continuing to lie to yourself will leave you exactly where you are.

It is a widely-spread meme today that we live in a world of me-ism. This is not an untrue observation about the ego in action. But of equal importance in this equation in the process of self-analysis is the factor of 'not me-ism'. The ego is great for convincing us that others are to blame for things and never ourselves. The mindset of 'not me-ism' is present in the mind of everyone controlled by the ego. This goes back to Jesus' parable about the splinter in another's eye and the plank in their own. 'Not me-ism' is the safe haven of personal denial, it is the basis of all psychological projection onto others the things we do and refuse to admit about our own ego habits and behaviors. On the road to cognitive advancement, one must rid their consciousness not only of the me-ism inherent in the ego's sense of its own desires and self-superiority, but we must also acknowledge and overcome the inherent 'not me-ism' that allows the ego to avoid responsibility for its own actions by projecting that blame on others.

Shakespeare wrote, "This above all: to thine own self be true." On the path to cognitive advancement and overcoming the ego, this saying is a mandate. One will not progress on this path if they continually allow the ego to lie to themselves about themselves. The self you must be true to is the inner self, what Nietzsche called the 'higher mind'. You will never find the higher mind of who you really are if you do not dedicate yourself to finding that higher mind and slay the false ego in the process.

Jesus taught that, "No one can serve two masters. Either you will hate the one and love the other, or you will be devoted to one and despise the other. Ye cannot serve God and mammon." In this passage God is the higher mind, the inner self, and mammon is the world of the ego. You cannot serve both for only one will rule your consciousness. Contrary to some common New Age and occult beliefs, you can't make a deal with the ego to create some sense of shared power within yourself. Such ideas are only one's ego equivocating in one's mind in order to maintain its control.

There is no sharing of power between who you really are and who the ego makes you think you are. They are two separate and mutually exclusive masters over your consciousness that, in the end, only one will rule. Whichever aspect of consciousness that you embrace as your ruler, then that is what will control your consciousness. As you think, so you are, as Buddha taught.

Each of us is faced with a choice on this path. There is the easy road, the one filled with quick denial and cognitive comfort, the world of cognitive me-ism and 'not me-ism', and the more difficult path of accepting the truth about ourselves, which is highly uncomfortable from a psychological standpoint until one comes out clean and free on the other side of their own personal dark abyss. Through tearing down the ego and removing its habits from our mind, we must all transition through our own 'dark night of the soul' to emerge from the other side. To make this journey and ultimately succeed, one must defeat fear, false clarity and the lure of ego power, as don Juan warned against being the three most powerful enemies that one must overcome on this road to freedom. To accomplish this feat, as stated previously, one must develop 'unbending intent', and develop a backbone of titanium to have the courage and stamina to cross that dark personal abyss. This is not a task taken on as a lark or a weekend hobby. It requires a supreme amount of personal discipline to walk this road, and an equal amount of patience, for this process is not suited for an instant gratification mindset.

This process takes commitment. Not a commitment to some belief system, but a commitment to oneself to continue with the process no matter the cost until the victory is achieved and your mind is totally free of the ego and its habits. Letting go of the beliefs from the external world that we have embraced is substantially easier than letting go of the beliefs we have accepted as the identity of the false ego. Nietzsche's collected works are a compendium of his own soul-searching, and the angst, depression, disenchantment and his ultimate victory of transcendence are catalogued in his works. They stand as an example of what this task entails with each of us having to come face to face with our own inner ego demon. His works present a *progression* toward an advanced state of consciousness. All too many philosophers accept the whole of Nietzsche's work as his 'philosophy', yet they represent varying stages of his own development.

As you progress on your own path, things you believe today will not be what you believe a year from now, or five years from now, or even ten. With the process of eroding and destroying the false ego, one's perceptions change. We all go into a state of cognitive flux where nothing seems permanent, and this gives rise to cognitive dissonance and psychological discomfort. In tearing down the illusion, this discomfort can't be avoided, nor should one seek to avoid it. The idea of permanency itself is just another illusion of the ego to create a sense of stability for this false world of illusion in which it lives.

Because of the hive nature of the virus, we have all come to believe that there must be some kind of one-size-fits-all solution for finding enlightenment. Due to the embedded nature of the hapiym group mind, we have all fallen prey to thinking that there should be just one way to achieve this enlightenment. This false perception had led to the creation of religions that all function and maintain their institutions through a form of groupthink. Regardless of the teachings of Buddha about the individual self, with institutionalized Buddhism we only find groupthink, with its adherents dressing alike and acting alike, no different than any other human herd. There is no individuality in these actions, only ego herd groupthink What a travesty this is to the idea of a free and independent consciousness taught by Buddha, and spit in his eye!

The path to cognitive freedom is an individual path because no two people are alike. They are not alike in their backgrounds, their early childhood, family life, education or cultural environments. They are each individual in their experiences; their joys as well as their personal physical and emotional traumas. All of these factors shape the ego false self, and as such, everyone's individual path is necessarily unique. The things I had to overcome on my path are not the things that you must overcome on yours. We may have some shared cultural programming, but how we each interpret that shared programming is going to be different.

I went to great lengths to describe this process of challenging and transcending the ego in my book *Demystifying the Mystical*. In composing that book I did my very best to offer guidelines for understanding this process to everyone. The book is by no means exhaustive in describing every lie the ego will tell us about ourselves, but it hits many of the high points that are the most common for all of us to transcend. Maybe with this understanding about your own individual ego, you can comprehend why this process can't be spelled out A, B, C. My path was mine just as your path is uniquely your own. There are certain shared beliefs that are commonalities, but when it comes to one's own internal work, we must each conquer our own egos. As all the teachers in the past have taught, only you can find you.

2,500 years ago, the world was less complicated. There were less cognitive harnesses than we have in our world today. We each carry the additional weight of cultural advancement that has given the ego persona many dimensions through which to expand its rule over our consciousness. This factor alone should bear consideration as to why Jesus and Buddha met with more success in their time than one faces today in this era of information overload and historical programming. The ego has gotten fat on this expansion, making our inner selves that much harder to find in our present generation. The weight of presumed knowledge, expanded religions, New Age mystical beliefs and false political ideals have only added more trash to the ego's cognitive rubbish heap, and all of that must be sifted through to find the truth buried deep in the ego's cognitive landfill.

In some respects, we may be the most informed generation where the overload of information to digest is concerned. But we are much further from finding our true selves as a result of being buried in this mountain of information. We do not have the simplicity of life that our predecessor teachers had to make their teachings more accessible for understanding. There has been too much willful psychological manipulation over the last century by those who have the money and power to control the public perceptions now more than any time in human history. Living with this truth makes this process that much harder for all of us.

As don Juan taught, the price for freedom is high, but it can be paid with diligence and courage and the unbending intent to succeed. This concept of unbending intent is what Nietzsche called the 'will to power'.

Although Nietzsche disclaimed being any kind of prophet, he did possess a vision of how things *could* be, just as Buddha envisioned a world where people are more compassionate with one another, and Jesus saw the brewing conflict when cognitive worlds collide, which would lead to an era of peace on Earth. Nietzsche's prophetic vision was that of what he called the overman, or Superman. Unfortunately, his vision of the superman has been turned to sewage through tyrants like Adolph Hitler, who interpreted his words from a strictly egoistic power-hungry perspective. Nietzsche never claimed that, even with his own state of cognitive advancement, that he was the overman. The Superman to come is what humanity *can* become once we transcend all this ego tyranny. The second cognition state of awareness is not an ending, a goal to be attained that is an end unto itself, but is a doorway to a *beginning*, through which, if humanity proceeds past it, will open the door to a state of human advancement that we can scarcely perceive from the current stagnant swamps of our perception.

I do not claim any more than Nietzsche did that I am his vision of the superman, but I have crossed that second cognition threshold far enough that I can see an unlimited future for humanity if it will but choose to embark on this journey and leave the illusionary world of the ego behind as nothing more than a bad memory. Where first cognition humanity is concerned, Buddha's concept of a compassionate world is one of obligation, where the ego must exhibit compassion to feel good about itself. In the second cognition state of awareness, compassion holds no such egotistical mandate, it becomes part of one's conscious choosing because it simply makes the most sense. One cannot mandate compassion any more than one can legislate morality, yet this is exactly how the first cognition world of the ego operates. The ego has no self-discipline, it only wants what it wants and damn anyone who gets in the way of that desire. If the ego exhibits compassion, it does so with an ulterior motive – to have bragging rights about how compassionate it is. Compassion as a state of being is a totally different concept which the ego cannot comprehend.

Of the overman, Nietzsche wrote in *Thus Spoke Zarathustra*:

> *"I teach you the overman. Man is something that shall be overcome. What have you done to overcome him?*

> *"All beings so far have created something beyond themselves; and do you want to be the ebb of this great flood and even go back to the beasts rather than overcome man? What is the ape to man? A laughingstock or a painful embarrassment. And man shall be just that for the overman: a laughingstock or a painful em-barrassment. You have made your way from worm*

to man, and much in you is still worm. Once you were apes, and even now, too, man is more ape than any ape.

"Man is a rope, tied between beast and overman - a rope over an abyss. A dangerous across, a dangerous on-the-way, a dangerous looking-back, a dangerous shuddering and stopping.

"What is great in man is that he is a bridge and not an end: what can be loved in man is that he is an overture and a going under.

"I love those who do not know how to live, except by going under, for they are those who cross over.

"I love the great despisers because they are the great reverers and arrows of longing for the other shore.

"I love those who do not first seek behind the stars for a reason to go under and be a sacrifice, but who sacrifice themselves for the earth, that the earth may some day become the overman's.

"I love him who lives to know, and who wants to know so that the overman may live some day. And thus he wants to go under.

"I love him who works and invents to build a house for the overman and to prepare earth, animal, and plant for him: for thus he wants to go under.

"I love him who loves his virtue, for virtue is the will to go under and an arrow of longing.

"I love him who does not hold back one drop of spirit for himself, but wants to be entirely the spirit of his virtue: thus he strides over the bridge as spirit."

What you each must decide on your own path is whether you are willing to settle for being the mask of a man, a hollow shell controlled by the ego, a true ghost in the machine, or whether you are willing to 'go under', to kill the false ego and come out the other side, to cross that abyss to discover who you really are. If you are one of those people, then Nietzsche left these words of encouragement to you:

*"In order to understand this type one must first realize the physiological precondition: it is what I call **great unhealthiness**. I do not know how*

*to explain this concept any better or **more personally** than I have already done in one of the final sections of the fifth book of the "gaya scienza." "We new, nameless, poorly understood ones" — it says there —, "we premature births of a future as yet unproved, we require for a new end a new means as well, namely, a new healthiness, a stronger, shrewder, tougher, bolder, merrier healthiness than any that has yet been. He whose soul thirsts to have experienced the whole range of hitherto existing values and desiderata and to have sailed around every coast of this ideal "Mediterranean," he who wants to know from the adventures of his own most personal experience how it feels to be a conqueror and discoverer of the ideal, as well as an artist, a saint, a lawgiver, a sage, a scholar, a pietist, a divine recluse of the old school: for that he needs one thing above all else, **great healthiness** — a healthiness one not only has but which one continually acquires and must acquire because one always relinquishes and must relinquish it...And now, after having been long underway in this way, we Argonauts of the ideal, more valiant perhaps than is prudent, and often enough shipwrecked and come to grief, but, as remarked, healthier than some would like to admit, dangerously healthy over and over again, — it would seem to us as if we have as a reward* *therefore a still undiscovered country before us, whose boundaries no one has yet seen, a land beyond all hitherto existing lands and cubbyholes of the ideal, a world so overly rich in things beautiful, unusual, questionable, terrible, and divine that our curiosity as well as our thirst for possession has gotten out of hand — alas, now nothing can satisfy us anymore!...With such outlooks before us and such a ravenous hunger in science and conscience, how could we still be satisfied with* **present-day men**? *This is bad enough, but it is inevitable that we should find it hard to maintain seriousness when looking upon his worthiest goals and hopes and perhaps not once looking upon them again...Another ideal runs ahead of us, a strange, seductive, danger-rich ideal to which we do not wish to persuade anyone because we do not easily allow anyone* **the right to it:** *the ideal of a spirit who naively, that is to say, unintentionally and out of an overflowing fullness and powerlessness, plays with all that was hitherto called holy, good, untouchable, godly; for whom the highest thing upon which the people rightly base their standard of value would already amount to a danger, a decay, a degradation, or, at the very least, a relaxation, a blindness, a temporary self-forgetting; the ideal of a human-superhuman well-being and well-wishing, which will often enough* *seem inhuman, for example, when placed next to all hitherto existing seriousness of this world, all hitherto existing solemnity of gesture, word, sound, look, morality, and task as their most incarnate and involuntary parody — and with which, despite all that, perhaps **the great seriousness** first commences, the actual note of interrogation is first set, the soul's destiny turns around, the clock-hand moves on, the tragedy begins...""*

[Emphasis in original]

The "great unhealthiness" of which Nietzsche writes is the sickness called ego. To reach that state of great cognitive healthiness, one must transcend and destroy this virus of the mind and every illusion it embraces and exchange it for truth. Those who embark on this journey for cognitive freedom are Nietzsche's "Argonauts", crossing a sea of uncertainty and doubt to arrive at a new land for humanity to dwell, without the illusionary poison of the world of the ego. Are you one of these Argonauts, one who can deal with the sobriety and "great seriousness" to embark on the task of seeking to elevate man into his potential as the overman? Do you have the courage to overcome the "great unhealthiness" of the poisoning ego and what it has done to man as a species with its world of illusion? Are you this 'new type' of human being who is willing to take on this task, starting with yourself, to create those new horizons?

Every act of creation is coupled with destruction. The ground must be cleared before any new edifice can be erected, and this stands true for you and your personal path. You cannot build that cognitive house with an unshakable foundation on rock until you destroy the old one built on sand first. This is what all these teachers taught in unison. Each of them envisioned a better world for humanity, and each of them knew, from crossing their own personal ego abyss, what lays on the other side and what potential it opens up for the advancement of an entire planetary species. I, too, see this vision with a clarity that the ego can only blind with philosophical speculation, mystical misperceptions and false intellectualism. This new world awaits all who make that perilous internal journey to get there. It will not be given away to anyone, it must be earned. There is only one thing left for anyone to do --- make a choice to start their own journey and stick with it through completion.

The Evolution of Consciousness Series

Book 1

A Philosophy for the Average Man: An Uncommon Solution to a World Without Common Sense by Endall Beall

Book 2

Willful Evolution: The Path to Advanced Cognitive Awareness and a Personal Shift in Consciousness by Endall Beall

Book 3

Demystifying the Mystical: Exposing Myths of the Mystical and the Supernatural by Providing Solutions to the Spirit Path and Human Evolution by Endall Beall

Book 4

Navigating into the Second Cognition: The Map for your journey into higher Conscious Awareness by Endall Beall

Book 5

The Energy Experience: Energy work for the Second Cognition by Mrs. Endall Beall

Book 6

We Are Not Alone – Part 1: Advancing Cognitive Awareness in an Interactive Universe by Endall Beall

Book 7

We Are Not Alone – Part 2: Advancing Cognitive Awareness through Historical Revelations - Endall Beall

Book 8

Advanced Teachings for the Second Cognition by Mrs. Endall Beall

Book 9

We Are Not Alone – Part 3: The Luciferian Agenda of the Mother Goddess by Endall Beall

Companion Volumes to The Evolution of Consciousness Series

False Prophecies, Reassessing Buddha and the Call to the Second Cognition by Endall Beall

Operator's Manual for the True Spirit Warrior by Endall Beall

Spiritual Pragmatism: A Practical Approach to Spirit Work in a World Controlled by Ego by Endall Beall

Revamping Psychology: A Critique of Transpersonal Psychology Viewed From the Second Cognition by Endall Beall & Mrs. Endall Beall

Second Cognition Series

Book 1

The New Paradigm Transcripts: Teachings for a New Tomorrow by Endall Beall & Doug Michael

Book 2

Breaking the Chains of the First Cognition: Tools for Understanding the Path to the Second Cognition by Endall Beall & Doug Michael

Book 3

PSOYCA – Road to the Second Cognition by Endall Beall & Doug Michael

Book 4

The Energetic War Against Humanity: The 6,000 Year War Against Human Cognitive Advancement by Endall Beall

Book 5

The Cognitive Illusion of History: How Humanity Has Been Controlled Through Selective and Biased Historical Reporting by Endall Beall & Doug Michael

In Progress –

Book 6

The Second Cognition Toolbox: Requirements for Advancing Your Consciousness by Endall Beall

Book 7

Firestarters: The Gemma and Endall Transcripts – by Endall Beall and Gemma Beall

Book 8

No Trespassing: Creating a New World Based on Mutual Respect by Endall Beall

Companion Volumes to the Second Cognition Series

Understanding Wisdom: A Treatise on Wisdom Viewed from the Second Cognition by Endall Beall

From Belief to Truth – From Truth to Wisdom by Endall Beall

Standalone Work: (In progress)

Clarifying the don Juan Teachings for the Second Cognition: A Pragmatic Reanalysis Without the Mystical Misdirection – by Endall Beall
(Upon completion, this volume will be offered as a free .pdf download from our website at *demystfyingthemystical.com* under the provisions of the Fair Use Doctrine as educational material.)

For questions or inquiries contact the authors at *Demystifyingthemystical.com.*